Art Director: Rodrigo Fino
Associate Editor: Steve Dorsey
Illustrator: Chris Morris
Editorial direction/production:
Maxine Marshall, Jonathan Jordan, Jen Glynn, Leah Pierre
Copy editing: Hayden Seder, Tonya Trybula
Author photograph by Enrique de Figueroa
Book cover and interior design by Rodrigo Fino
Images: Credits appear on page 230

US$29.95
ISBN 978-1-966629-95-5

ISBN-13: 978-1-966629-95-5
52995
9 781966 629955

RIVER GROVE
BOOKS
www.rivergrovebooks.com

CONSULTING WITH HEART

The Power of Passion and the Stories That Shaped My Career

Mario García

Dedications

With gratitude to every client who ever put their faith in me. And even more, my love and eternal gratitude to my late wife, Maria, and my four children—Mario, Brian, Ana, and Elena—for allowing me to follow my heart and passion.

Table of contents

Lessons from the Tortugas

My fascination with turtles (*tortugas* in Spanish) began in my childhood in Cuba, that beautiful Caribbean island surrounded by the bluest of turquoise waters—and home to a surprising variety of turtles. I vividly remember a family trip to Cienfuegos, a city on the southern coast of Cuba, where I first encountered the most exotic of all Cuban turtles: the rare red-footed tortoise. With its striking red-and-orange markings, it was a creature of wonder.

As a child, I was mesmerized by the deliberate way turtles moved—slow but purposeful, always making progress only when they extended their heads beyond the safety of their shells. That quiet perseverance left an impression, one that would become deeply symbolic years later when I arrived in the United States as a refugee at the age of fourteen.

Ironically, my relationship with turtles took an unexpected turn decades later, when my late wife, Maria, and I purchased a beautiful lot along the Hillsborough River in Tampa, Florida. It was the perfect place to build our dream home. The architect delivered an exciting, contemporary design, complete with a swimming pool and spa, that exceeded all our expectations. "From the front door," he promised, "you'll see the shimmering blue of the pool, then the lush green waters of the river beyond." It sounded perfect.

But the turtles had other plans.

Environmental authorities visited the site and, upon inspection, declared most of our backyard an ecologically protected wetland. Turtle nests had been discovered throughout the area. The plans had to be redrawn. The pool was pushed off to the side. The dream layout was no longer possible. At first, we were disappointed. But then something shifted.

We embraced the turtles.

We named our home *Villa Tortuga*. A dear artist friend from Mexico crafted a beautiful ceramic turtle to place at the entrance of the house. And as we settled in, we often watched the turtles wander across our backyard, their calm movements a daily reminder of nature's quiet wisdom. Over time, my fascination turned into a collection—glass turtles, wooden turtles, ceramic ones of every shape and size. Friends began to bring me turtles from their travels: I soon had Israeli, Mexican, and Thai turtles sharing space on my shelves.

I admire the way turtles retreat when the noise gets too loud—only to reemerge, head forward, moving ahead on their own terms.

That image offers a perfect metaphor for the journey we are all on as we face the era of artificial intelligence. To understand AI, we, too, must sometimes withdraw—pause, reflect, and absorb the monumental wave of information coming at us daily. But then, we must also dare to stick our heads out of our shells, to explore, to question, and to move forward—curious, cautious, but determined to discover what this transformative technology can do for us.

Villa Tortuga, Hillsborough River, Tampa, FL—1988

The turtle with the best color palette is definitely the Cuban red-footed tortoise.

Appreciations

While it may not take a village to get a book like this published, it does require the talents and skills of several people whose coordinated effort and support helped the author reach the finish line. I am lucky to be surrounded by such people. While I was not planning to write another book, the book apparently wanted to write itself. I was on a flight from Zurich to New York on June 12, 2024, and while my eyes were set on the snow-covered mountains of the Swiss Alps–that fabulous sight when you take off from the Zurich airport–my head was on a different set of clouds, dictating to me the words that would be the beginning of this book.

Upon landing, I remember typing notes to myself about a possible book on consulting. The first person I shared any of this with was Steve Dorsey, a colleague whose stellar work in the media business I have long respected and one of those unusual journalism types who is well versed on the journalistic and visual side of the business and quite adept with technology. If the author of this book was going to count on a copilot who could understand that any content created today is a fusion of journalism/design/technology, then that would be Steve. He was enthusiastic about the idea of this book from day one, and so he was my collaborator: reading my first messy manuscript, providing ideas for moving paragraphs and chapters around, suggesting experts I could tap into to enhance the content. Every day for months, Steve would surprise me with another of his famous "What if you . . . " emails and texts. For almost all of those what-ifs, I responded with a "why not."

So, I could not have produced this book without the continued and robust support of Steve Dorsey, to whom I am grateful.

However, the first thing that a reader sees is the design of the book. I could not think of anyone but our own Garcia Media senior art director, Rodrigo Fino, for the task of designing **Consulting with Heart**. Rodrigo Fino has worked with me since his graduation from college three decades ago. I blink and he already knows that I want the headline larger or bolder. I say little and Rodrigo knows that perhaps he needs to present another idea. Such are our professional dynamics. Rodrigo is trained in graphic arts but has accompanied me on hundreds of redesign and transformation projects around the globe. He knows how people read. He also knows that less is best. What a blessing to have him creating the look of the book.

Speaking of visuals, the illustrations in the book represent the content in a single image for each chapter. There's nobody better than editorial illustrator Christopher Morris, (chrismorrisillustration.com), whose illustrations have appeared in some of the most distinguished US publications. Chris and I communicated about the content of each chapter. From the start, Chris knew what I wanted to say, the emphasis on heart and passion—and butterflies and turtles! This book is conversational, part memoir and part helpful guide for those contemplating a career in consulting. Chris caught the humorous moments of the narrative, and from his very first sketches, I could see that he'd captured the spirit of the book. So, thanks to Chris for sharing his talent with me and my readers here.

All content benefits from the extra set of eyes that comes from an editor. My heartfelt thanks to two Greenleaf editors, Jonathan Jordan and Hayden Seder, who enhanced the content by suggesting structural changes, staying vigilant for the presentation of factual material, and, of course, checking for grammar and spelling.

So, while I may not have needed a village to get this book to you, I think I visited the village and was able to recruit its most talented and generous residents to join me here. One thing every consultant already knows: Surround yourself with talented people, and everyone shines.

Foundations

Part 1

Introduction

I t was one of those celebratory moments a consultant dreams about: my first day at **The Wall Street Journal**, in 2000, for the start of a big project that would add color to this iconic financial daily. At 8:30 a.m., I was taking the elevator to where my first meeting would be. By 9:15, I had sketched a drawing of how I would propose color use on the front page.

The art director looked at it and said, "This will never fly here. Too much color." By 9:45, the CEO of the company stopped by to say hello, looked at my sketch, and said: "This is the way to go with color." The art director tried to smile. I shook the hand of the CEO and wished that the scheduled coffee break could turn into a champagne happy hour moment.

During my coffee break at Battery Park downstairs, I soaked in the views around me. The Statue of Liberty. An organ grinder–complete with his monkey–churning out tinny notes. It was a moment of consulting bliss–wanting to thank the Statue of Liberty for taking a Cuban refugee like me into the country, and the CEO for his seal of approval.

Moments like this haven't always been the norm, though. In 1997, I was in Hamburg, Germany, working on **Die Zeit,** the most difficult project of my career. After completing ten rounds of prototypes, I was still not showing anything that the client liked. Sometimes the consultant becomes collateral damage because of issues surrounding the engagement: A major publishing house had recently bought **Die Zeit,** and many of the journalists in the team were not too happy about the new business arrangement. It was the new owner who had handpicked me to redesign this iconic newspaper. While the owner did not attend any presentations in front of a hostile group, I was the face of the project and thus represented all that was negative in the eyes of the journalists.

Of course, there are those days–and those projects–when finding anything positive is as elusive as hailing a taxi on a snowy night in Manhattan. In my diary I wrote:

This project is steering me away from the "Positive Mario" mode and into a sour, frustrating mood and I am even contemplating quitting the project, throwing in the towel and deciding that there are projects that are not meant to be, should not be, and may even be harmful to your emotional health. Indeed, how can one attempt to recreate ten different concepts, facing rejection along the way. Ten rejections later, I think I am done. The editors in this project think that an American design consultant could never capture German elegance. I begin to ask myself: Can I do that? It takes a special effort to remain focused and positive, especially after you walk in from lunch one day and see a note stuck to your computer screen that reads: "Go home!"

Be prepared for those days when nothing you have ever done prepares you for the feeling of rejection, the type that makes you wonder about your own preparation for the task at hand—am I an impostor here posing as an expert? Fortunately, these feelings are ephemeral. A large portion of a consultant's day-to-day is a combination of learning new things, discovering skills you did not know you possessed, and adding notes to the chapter of your career that deals with getting to know the human condition.

Acceptance and rejection. Bliss or frustration. Those two moments of my consulting career encapsulate what the business of consulting can be all about. Anyone not ready to deal with those moments of utter frustration and outright rejection of their ideas should reconsider a career in consulting. Indeed, we advise, facilitate, and interpret dreams—sometimes with more success than others. In the process of interpreting the client's dreams, we sometimes puncture our own. While most of us think the ideas we are presenting to the client are nothing short of brilliant, not all are. Don't get too attached to your initial ideas—brilliant as they may be—and keep an open mind and ears. Many times, someone on the in-house project team has a better idea that is more suitable to the realities the project faces. After hundreds of projects, I've had more bliss than rejection—thank God—and I still believe we consultants have the best jobs: We don't report to the same office every day, we arrive as experts with people listening to us, and, when successful, we elevate the level of production for our client and become transformation agents.

What's a Consultant?

If you Google the word *consultant*, dozens of entries appear, not to mention references to books and guides about how to become a consultant. Most will tell you that a consultant helps a firm improve its performance, analyze its practices, change those practices when necessary, and provide specialized expertise. The consultant is a coach, an expert. The most successful ones are game changers. All these titles are worthy attributes for those who execute to perfection.

Of course, unlike accountants or even barbers, consultants are not regulated or required to have a license. As a result, many professionals call themselves consultants. Some truly are doing the job of the consultant—and some are not. My travel agent refers to himself as a "cruise consultant." Indeed, he is, and we, his clients, benefit from his advice before we pack to hit the high seas. I am always amused when my twenty-something graduate students tell me, "I'd like to be a consultant like you." Mind you, these are students who have not worked full-time in a media organization yet, but the title "consultant" appeals.

Ultimately, even though anyone can claim the title, impactful consultants need to bring added value to the situation through some element or combination of rich experience, unique perspective, or another ability that helps the client level up.

When our clients hire us, they are jumping into uncharted territory. Yes, there is a shiny proposal, a portfolio of work done by the consultant for other clients, and the promise of a sterling project carried to a successful completion. You can hear the champagne flutes clinking in anticipatory celebration! But there is inherent risk in the consultancy equation–the client is showing good faith that you will deliver results they could not achieve without you. The real test of the consultant's worth starts when he lands on the premises and begins to offer his experience and expertise. Most importantly, how does the consultant relate to the in-house team? First, the consultant listens. Second, he studies every aspect of the organization and its people, anticipating needs and evaluating the goals of the project. Each new client is taking a risk on the consultant, expecting great results.

DEFINITIONS.
What many definitions of *consultant* don't mention is that the consultant who penetrates an organization also plays other roles:

· **Father confessor:** The moment you arrive, key players and political animals jockey for position to tell you "their" side of the story. Everyone swears to secrecy and tells you, "What I am telling you today will become obvious, but I wanted you to be on alert. I have been here a long time. I know where all the bodies are buried."

· **Hand-holder:** Many of the execs who hire you are full of insecurities and will expect you to lead them by the hand through the project, coming in to rescue them from time to time by masking their inefficiencies and providing solutions, usually just in the nick of time (like during a presentation). They will remind you to be their advocate through statements like "Make sure you tell my boss that I do know what is going on here."

· **Validator:** Early enough in a project, what the consultant has not yet realized is that two or three key people will expect you to present their views, sometimes verbatim, to their superiors. They all chant in unison: "When you say it, it carries weight. When we do, it goes nowhere." I am always amazed that what they want to sell to their superiors makes perfect sense, but because the people who are doing the sales pitch do not pick their battles and fight for everyone, their superiors stop listening.

• **Talent scout:** As a consultant, you have been hired to deal with information and organizational design issues. Soon enough, you realize that people are not working to their full potential, so you immediately identify talents that could be better utilized. You tell the person who is supervising this talented individual, and usually, they are totally surprised that you would single this person out as outstanding. While I am not a management consultant nor a personnel director, I can tell you that two of the worst crimes committed in the newsrooms of the world is (1) when someone is not fired and (2) when talent is not allowed to advance within the ranks. It's moments like this when you need a consultant the most—you can spell C-O-N-S-U-L-T-A-N-T with all capital letters. You must approach this like a detective. Don't go by the official list of who is who. Review the workplace and make up your own list of who is talented—that one practice usually pays off. Talents are not necessarily at the top of a supervisor's list, and we all know that. Several times in my career I have had a publisher/editor tell me, "You need to find us an art director. We don't have anyone in house who can do it," only for me to turn around and prove them wrong by identifying a talented person out of total anonymity. Suddenly, they are rescued from a boring position and transferred into a realm where they can reveal their talents.

Roger Black is the executive chair and type consultant for **Type Network** and a former design director for such publications as **Rolling Stone, The New York Times,** and **Newsweek.** In an email he sent me, he highlighted the moment he realized he was doing consulting work, even though that was not his official title:

In 1987, after being a serial (and chief) director at Rolling Stone, The New York Times, and Newsweek, I realized that what I was doing was consulting. I liked going into a new publication, getting to know new people, and designing a new "format" that would work for them—and for their readers. It always ends with the readers, the end-users, the customers of a publication, or a site or an app. If they don't like it, don't find it useful and enjoyable, then it's a bad design. [1]

CONSULTING: A GROWING PROFESSION.

According to **IBISWorld,** the global management consulting industry employed approximately 6.8 million people in 2024, reflecting a 3.5 percent increase from the previous year. (2)

They form a diverse array of professionals working in various sectors such as management, IT, financial services, health care, media transformation, and more.

Management consultants, IT consultants, and those focusing on digital transformation are among the most prominent groups. However, consulting roles can vary widely in terms of responsibilities and work environments. The consulting market is experiencing rapid growth, driven by increasing digitalization and the demand for specialized expertise. A report from **Spherical Insights & Consulting** estimates that the global consulting service market was valued at $327.65 billion in 2023 and is projected to reach $494.36 billion by 2033. (3)

Like many other professions, consultants face the threat of some aspects of their jobs being taken over by technological advances. According to a Runn study, management consulting has a 27 percent chance of being automated. (4)

In addition, work-life balance is a problem for consultants, some of whom work fifty to eighty hours per week to cover the demands of their consultancy. When you are in a consulting role, it is easy to lose track of the hours you put in. The 2020 pandemic accelerated a new remote-work-heavy society, which has made the issue more complicated. I am thankful for my wonderful family, who supported me when making those adjustments. What I don't miss are the costly flights I had to take to get to a child's recital or graduation on time.

The field of consulting is growing and evolving. Changes in all fields are happening at an incredibly rapid pace. In many workplaces, there is more than one transformation taking place simultaneously.

We have every reason to believe that the work of experienced consultants will be in great demand as clients continue to accelerate their digital business transformation and adaptation to artificial intelligence (AI)—which we cover more extensively later in this book.

SAVE IT
Wear Many Hats

Your expertise may be in subjects A and C, but as a consultant, you will find yourself rapidly forced to develop other specialties, all of which have to do with the human condition and the people dynamics inside an organization. There are no consulting jobs where you will not have to navigate the in-house human dramas. Be a good listener, don't take sides, and inspire the team.

DRIVEN BY PASSION.

Passion drives action, while the heart guides direction. Together, they have enabled me as a consultant to make a positive impact, not only on the business, but also on the people within the organizations with which I have had the honor to collaborate. Consulting is a people business.

Those personal interactions play a major role in how a project will turn out. Passion and heart are two main ingredients to make a good mojito. The other two ingredients are expertise and experience.

EXPERTISE + Experience + **Passion** + Heart = **CONSULTANT**

CONSULTING IS IN YOUR FUTURE.

"You are about to become a consultant," said John Zeien, my colleague at Miami-Dade College. The year was 1976, and this was the first time I had heard the word *consultant* used in relation to myself. We were having coffee, just after I had finished teaching my Journalism 101 class, one of my duties as advisor to student publications. John was brainstorming ideas for Homecoming celebrations since he was director of student activities.

As usual, he was smoking his pipe that morning, and swirls of smoke moved in my direction as I relayed how **The Miami Herald** had contacted me to help its team with some layout ideas for their upcoming big project, the creation of a Spanish daily edition, **el Nuevo Herald.**

"Well, maybe consulting is in your future, and you should pursue it," John observed. I did not think much of his words, except that I shared my enthusiasm to be back in the Miami Herald building, enraptured by its grand views of beautiful Biscayne Bay, where I had done my journalism internship only a few years before. I remember the excitement I felt about the prospect of creating a new newspaper, of returning to work in a newsroom where I would acquire those real-life experiences that, in turn, would make me a better journalism instructor.

This moment was the beginning of the two roles that have become my career—consulting and teaching. To this day, my job as an educator is always fortified by the consulting work I do, the synchronizing of theory and practice. I can't imagine one without the other. The combination still allows me to offer my journalism students examples of what is happening in the real world and to wear my professorial hat when teaching in-house workshops for practicing journalists. An effective consultant should always be teaching.

PERSONAL NOTE
My First Consulting Job

el Nuevo Herald introduced me to the first "consultancy," light as it was. My role was to view prototypes that had been created internally and make recommendations about a possible logo. The late Carlos Castañeda, a Cuban journalist who had worked with **LIFE** Magazine's Spanish edition in Havana, created the original look of the newspaper. I came years later, in the late 1980s, to lead the first redesign, which included playing with the logo with its pink flamingo, the representation of tropical Miami. By then I already knew what a consultant was and had learned to use the term in my correspondence when offering my services.

Of course, at this stage in my young career, I was asking myself the question, Do I have what it takes to be a consultant? If the help provided by consultants is based upon those two key ingredients of expertise and experience, then I really did not possess those essentials for what Samir Parikh refers to as the "basic consulting proposition." (5)

I guess what I lacked in expertise and experience I compensated for in this other thing called self-assurance—and youthful courage—which will help you as a new consultant. Also, I had an abundance of passion, which pushed me to attempt tasks not yet on my resume. (By the way, prepare yourself for many mentions of passion.) I should add that the way consulting worked in 1976 is not exactly how it looks today. Despite my firm's fifty-plus years of consulting experience, new clients today insist on seeing our most recent work, and, specifically, how it applies to the proposed project we are pitching. For example: "Can you send us links to news websites you have transformed recently?" A good consultant is transparent and will provide the requested information in a clear, professional way. We will discuss this in more detail when we write about "the pitch." In Hollywood, they often say that an actor or director is only as good as her last project. The same applies to consultants today. ↪

↪ **IT WAS ANOTHER WORLD.** That first minor gig with **The Miami Herald** sparked a long trajectory that took me from city to city, country to country, continent to continent, newsroom to newsroom—a journey that has not quite ended yet. As I write this segment, I sit in Dusseldorf, Germany, ready to conduct a mobile storytelling and AI workshop for the team of the financial daily **Handelsblatt.** With every project come discoveries and constant new learning. Passion channels transformation and reinvention. Effective consultants teach themselves, as well as others. Each project leads to greater expertise and satisfaction •

MAKE A NOTE
Be Open to the Possibility

You never know when a call or email could offer you a passport to consulting. Nothing prepares you for the moment, but everything you have ever done is your resume. Be open to the possibilities. If you don't have the expertise yet, remember, you don't have to be the ultimate expert. You just need to start, be flexible, and turn every action into a lesson.

THE CONSULTANT AS INFLUENCER.

Now we can turn to the more practical and contemporary definitions of the word *consultant*. In its simplest terms, a consultant is someone who offers advice and practical solutions for clients who seek such help. If we use a trendier term, effective consultants are going to be "influencers," bringing their experience and expertise to stimulate change and transformation.

In her book about consulting, Linda K. Stroh defines the role of the consultant as follows: "A consultant is defined as someone who either advises a client on the desirability of taking some action, or who assists the client in making a decision and then helps the client in planning or implementing action as determined by the client. Several points are stated or implied by this definition." (6)

In *The Consulting Bible: How to Launch and Grow a Seven-Figure Consulting Business,* Alan Weiss states that "perhaps 90 percent of people calling themselves information technology (IT) consultants are, in reality, just paid help without the benefits." He adds: "A consultant is a 'brain,' a subcontractor is another 'pair of hands.'" (7)

INTERPRETER OF DREAMS.

There are countless books available about what consulting is, but what those books don't mention is that the consultant is an interpreter of dreams. This metaphorical role—interpreter of dreams—encapsulates the essence of consulting, where our clients present their goals, visions, or "dreams," and we consultants work to translate these into actionable plans and tangible results.

In my experience, the first briefing meeting is where the client and the project group put their dreams on the table. For example, in our own practice, that's the moment when the client envisions how color or a new look should attract younger readers or how toning down those bold primary colors on the front page or home page can give the publication a greater sense of gravitas. More recently, I find myself translating the dream of digital transformation into a step-by-step road map, encompassing content strategy, technology adoption, and staff training. This might involve recommending new content management systems, designing mobile-friendly websites, and implementing social media strategies. Often, this will move people in key roles within the organization. For sure, interpreting the dream is easier than executing it into reality.

Interpreting a client's dream means bridging the gap between vision and execution. For example, a tech start-up dreams of launching a groundbreaking new product. The consultant must bridge the gap between the visionary idea and its execution. The consultant works closely with the start-up team, ensuring that the product design, development, and marketing efforts are aligned with the overall vision. The consultant brings the outsider's perspective or ideal customer perspective to identify any pitfalls or blind spots in the plan. They might also facilitate partnerships and secure funding.

This includes such reality steps as:
• Conducting market research to validate the product concept
• Developing a go-to-market strategy
• Creating detailed project plans with timelines and milestones

As interpreters of dreams, we bring in our experience and expertise. For example, consider a company that dreams of becoming more agile and responsive to market changes. The consultant helps the company transition from a hierarchical structure to a more flexible, team-based approach.

They might introduce agile methodologies, provide training, and offer ongoing support to ensure the changes are sustainable. The consultant provides the necessary expertise to restructure the organization, which involves the following actions:
- Assessing the current organizational structure
- Recommending changes to improve efficiency and flexibility
- Implementing new processes and systems

Sometimes the client's dreams require major change and innovation. For example, a retail company dreams of integrating AI to enhance customer experience.

The consultant guides the company through the AI integration process, from selecting the right AI tools to training employees on their use. It's our job as consultants to ensure that the implementation aligns with the company's vision of enhanced customer engagement and operational efficiency. The consultant facilitates this innovation by
- Identifying areas where AI can add value
- Developing AI strategies and implementation plans
- Managing the change process and ensuring stakeholder buy-in

Finally, a consultant is there to empower clients to achieve their dreams. It is one of the most satisfying aspects of the consultant's role. Each project is unique, but the underlying process of interpreting and realizing dreams remains constant. This role requires a blend of empathy, creativity, and strategic thinking, making consultants indispensable in the business world.

Sometimes the dream is of an unrealistic scope. For example, when a client publisher of a weekly regional newspaper tells me, *"I would like for us to go digital a la The New York Times."*

Dreaming big is a good starting point, but localizing that dream to the realities of available resources is a practical necessity. The consultant in this case must walk that thin line of not stopping the client's big dream while outlining parts of it that can be achieved during the course of this project and drafting a timeline to execute other parts of it in the future. When a regional newspaper publisher and amateur chef wanted to create a cooking app in the style of the much-celebrated

"Cooking" section of **The New York Times**, I applauded the decision but directed the team to first start building an archive of the hundreds of recipes already published in the past sixty years. This allowed for the big dream to exist within the realistic boundaries of the organization.

While I usually get a clear idea of what the client's dream is by the end of that first meeting with the project team, I never leave the room without asking one question: "When you close your eyes and envision how this product will look at the end of this project, what do you see?"

That's a revealing moment. I make mental notes, then hurry to my iPhone to jot down essential thoughts that should not escape. In my experience, 75 percent of what the client envisions for the product is translated to the final version. Experience and expertise—along with vision—drive the process of interpreting your clients' dreams.

PERSONAL NOTE
How I See Mysef

I see myself as someone who sells ideas, interprets dreams, and is often the writer for what Jony Ive (the genius behind Apple's greatest products) refers to as "the biography of an idea." (8)

The moment of birth for an idea is usually via a discussion on that first important meeting when the client expresses her desires, and I, as a consultant, dig into my experience and expertise to find how I can deliver them. It's always struck me how Apple emphasizes the care and attention they put into understanding and nurturing the essence of an idea during their product development process.

As an agent of change and transformation and facilitator of the conversation, I pack innovation in my backpack, along with my MacBook Air and my Moleskine notebook. I cherish my role as interpreter of dreams, who is there at the end of the project, when the new product is launched, to experience the clients enjoying the results. The consultant's reward is that moment when she translates the vision of the client into a set of concrete realities.

Consider digital transformation, where dreams of technological prowess and seamless content delivery take flight. The consultant, much like a dream interpreter, deciphers these aspirations and molds them into a step-by-step road map—a living, breathing guide that encompasses content strategy, technology adoption, and the meticulous training of staff. Each recommendation, be it a cutting-edge content management system, $\longrightarrow$

↪ a mobile-friendly design, or a robust social media strategy, is a brushstroke on the canvas of the client's dream. But interpreting the dream is but one facet of the journey. Executing it, transmuting vision into reality, is where the true success of the project lies. It is here that the consultant must wield the tools of the trade with precision and passion, navigating the delicate balance between the dream and the tangible, often orchestrating changes in the very fabric of the organization. This is when the consultant stands as both artist and craftsman, translating the ineffable into the actionable, and in doing so, becomes a true interpreter of dreams. This role is essential in the job of the consultant •

GREAT IDEA
Consultants Play Many Roles

When a consultant arrives to help a client, he opens himself to serve in a variety of roles, some of which have nothing to do with his expertise. Some of these roles include father confessor, hand-holder, validator, facilitator, talent scout, and interpreter of dreams. Oh yes, the consultant is also expected to deliver the project for which he was contracted.

HOW TO DEVELOP A CONSULTING BUSINESS.
Developing a consulting business is not as simple as renting office space, setting up the computer, designing a catchy logo, and, presto, a new consultancy is born. In fact, if there is a profession where the process of evolutionary steps is key, that will be consulting.

So you want to be a consultant, and you have tested your skills within the limited confines of a single firm, where you have excelled with your ability to listen and to find solutions to problems that confounded your peers. As a result, your superiors have chosen you to represent the company at conferences where you have also excelled in your ability to get in front of groups to present your ideas successfully. By now you know that you can spot problems, offer solutions, get results, and then present case studies for others in your field. Looks like you have the essentials to become a consultant.

The fact that you now have covered the essentials, however, does not mean that you are ready to leave your full-time job and open your own consulting business. Don't leave your day job until you have tested the water with a couple of freelance consulting jobs. Personally, I delayed creating my own consulting firm, **García Media,** for years, since my wife and I had four children to educate, and my full-time teaching jobs provided steady income and health insurance. As more consulting jobs appeared—it was the golden age of newspaper redesigns during the 1980s and '90s, and publishers wanted to add color and pizzaz to their titles—I decided that it was time for **García Media.** A logo was designed and office space secured, and eventually there would be offices of García Media in Buenos Aires and Hamburg, too.

Then the real work began, helping media organizations with their timely transformations. With the success of each new job, other clients would appear. That is still the primary source of new clients for **García Media** today. A great source of pride for me rests in the fact that 60 percent of my business is return business. Some of my clients have been working with me for three decades or more, with various challenges brought about by technological advances, as well as changes in consumer behavior and how we consume news and information today. For me, the formula to getting the name/brand out there is a combination of:

- Writing blogs/articles (my blog is at garciamedia.com)
- Speaking at events
- Publishing books

When you first start consulting, you have not yet achieved name recognition, as you will once you develop a portfolio of successful consulting projects. Conferences are key to achieving such recognition. Conferences come in all sizes, too. My early speaking engagements happened at small gatherings of regional press leaders, often in a scenic remote location, but attended by enough potential clients. I drove my station wagon through many snowy roads in upstate New York, and sometimes into Canada, to speak at conferences for small daily and weekly newspapers. Sometimes one of those conferences would yield two or three contacts, one developing into a project. Sometimes, the contact would come months after the actual conference. I would print my cards—those were the days when a handshake and the business card would be the first connection with a potential client. Those conferences also usually provided audience questions and interactions reflecting universal themes that I could turn into an article, which I would pitch to a media journal, thus amplifying the reach, extending the name recognition, and, quite often, leading to exchanges with potential clients.

The new consultant must gain exposure. Speaking at conferences, participating in panels, and standing out with unique ideas that resonate with those in the audience are key. In my case, dealing with newspaper design, the critique of poor color use could be described as "wearing your best Carmen Miranda hat," which always brought the house down with laughter, but the point was made: Your newspaper abuses color. On a more serious note, I often used the term *Center of Visual Impact* to teach newspaper editors about the importance of visual hierarchy. Even decades later, those references are mentioned and referred to as "García-isms." I am honored, but they were not meant for posterity.

Promote yourself—nobody can do it better. I tell my students to never go to bed without asking the question, What did I do today to promote myself and my work? It could be an email you wrote, a social media post that you put together with an image of your work, a thought left on LinkedIn, that call you made. In the words of Alan Weiss, "Become cited and quoted, and (perhaps inappropriately at times) be considered the final word or authority on a subject." (9)

Don't forget social media: I use social media daily to promote my blog posts, my books, and my speaking engagements. Books and speeches whet the appetite of prospective clients effectively. Publish case studies of your completed projects. Don't be afraid to give away some of your tips and suggestions—there is much more where that came from. "The books, speeches, postings, citations, attributions, and a plethora of interactions near and far only serve to make the thought leader more sought, not less." (10)

QUALITIES OF A GOOD CONSULTANT.
No one prepared me to turn into a consultant. Instead, that first **Miami Herald** engagement landed me in the role of consultant without much previous preparation. As I rode the elevator at One Herald Plaza, I saw the floor numbers change and had the space of a three-floor journey to remind myself that I could do this. Excitement about the prospect of a new

project always dominated over that stirring in the middle of my stomach. Decades later, I still have those same feelings of excitement and a bit of trepidation as I approach the first meeting for a project. In the baptism-by-fire rituals that have been such a part of my professional life, I have learned a few lessons that have served me well while acting as a consultant:

- The consultant builds teams.
- The consultant is a guest in the house.
- The consultant offers advice, presents options, and enhances the dialogue but does not dominate it.
- The consultant becomes a partner in a learning process, not someone who imposes ideas.
- The consultant treats each project as if it was his first, borrowing from previous experiences but always making sure that the existing project reflects uniqueness.
- The consultant must pretend that he/she is part of the team, works full time with them, and does not mix one project with the other.
- The consultant is a change agent.
- The consultant is a validator of ideas that are already existing within the in-house project team.

GREAT IDEA
The Importance of Marketing

Nothing beats a good performance that leads to word-of-mouth recommendations from one client to another. However, the effective, busy consultant uses every possible avenue to promote her work and to let prospective clients know about the success of completed projects. In my case, I always write a blog post about the case study of a just-completed project, offering details and also including how the audience the product was created for reacted to the change. I accept invitations to speak at conferences where prospective clients gather and then incorporate project case studies in the presentation. Also, write articles and books. Words are powerful tools to advance your work.

The First Project Is a Game Changer

The first consulting project I had outside of my "neighborhood" of upstate New York happened in freezing Minnesota with the redesign of the St. Cloud Daily Times in 1979. Thanks to an eagle, the project put me on the map. This was no ordinary American eagle. This was an American eagle with wings expanding about eight columns across the top of the page, serving as the centerpiece. This was an eagle that when we changed its design to a more stylized eagle, it grew bigger wings that took off with me under them. The flight of that eagle has been a journey that has not ended for me yet.

The first time I laid eyes on a copy of the **Daily Times,** I knew we had to get that eagle off the front page. Perhaps it happens to other consultants, regardless of the subject matter, but somehow you identify the aspect of the project that must be tackled no matter what. In my case here, it was the eagle. On rare occasions, that first jolt of "this must change" refers to the human element. Someone in a position of power immediately appears as a person who will not help the consultant advance the project. A couple of times I have remarked to my clients: "We should not start this project until you have the right people in the right spots." That was not the case in St. Cloud.

To make matters worse, this ugly eagle was literally wrapped around an American flag. Branding is key for a company's image and even more so for daily newspapers. Familiarity is important for people who welcome the same newspaper into their homes daily, in many places through generations. As a result, how a newspaper's name is presented at the top of the front page becomes a key element of every project. Changing it is often a no-no that is specified in the briefing: Don't tamper with the logo!

You must remember that this was my first official redesign project from start to finish. In the process, I learned valuable lessons, most importantly: Yes, you can push for what you believe in, and sometimes you accomplish what everyone around you thinks is not possible.

At the time, I was a professor at Syracuse University's S.I. Newhouse School of Public Communications—and while reviewing some old notes, I found my reference to St. Cloud's nameplate eagle: " . . . most importantly, the front-page nameplate displayed a spreading and graphically overwhelming eagle, which became the greatest source of irritation and delays as we proceeded with our redesign efforts."

Around 1978, the young staff of the **Daily Times,** led by news editor John Bodette (retired), had formed a "redesign committee" that spent

SUNDAY, May 22, 1988

St. Cloud Times 75¢

127th Year 295   Copyright 1988 St Cloud Newspapers Inc   A Gannett Newspaper   St. Cloud, Minnesota 56302

St.Cloud Times

SATURDAY, JUNE 14, 2025 | SCTIMES.COM   PART OF THE USA TODAY NETWORK

The evolution of the St. Cloud Daily Times.

months meeting regularly, analyzing the newspaper, and trying to come up with graphic ideas to improve the appearance. But Bodette and the Times editor at the time, Don Casey, soon realized that their in-house efforts to redesign the paper were hampered by a lack of direction. Their realization prompted them to seek an outside opinion, at which point I became involved with the Times as a design consultant.

I asked Bodette to send me two weeks' worth of newspapers to analyze. This allowed me to observe the newspaper's highs and lows, as well as grasp a basic understanding of the newspaper's regular day-to-day news content, photo selections and art choices, and the role of visual journalism in how the newspaper was put together daily.

By the time I made my first visit to St. Cloud–a snowy day, of course –I was able to experience the gravitational center of the city, the locale where readers and advertisers of this newspaper lived. At the time, St. Cloud had a population of about 44,000, and I soon realized that the city was close enough to Minneapolis that it was like a microcosm of the larger city. This mental image floated in my head, leading me to think that the old, ugly eagle on the nameplate could be replaced with something more stylish.

EVIL EAGLE THOUGHTS.
The transformation started with me sketching a modern version of this eagle on napkins, business cards, and anything else I could use a pencil on. It became a crusade for me, but I was still not telling anyone about these controversial thoughts. How do you begin a project–your first, at that–by informing the editors you want to change the nameplate and, furthermore, remove a patriotic symbol as strong as an American eagle? I later found out that the American eagle was a major nameplate staple of newspapers across the country.

I was also aware that as a Cuban American, many in the newsroom might see me as someone with no real patriotic feelings or attachments to this American symbol of freedom. But within me, I knew the paper would be more dynamic, more appealing, if the nameplate/eagle was removed. Less is more. Something had to be done. There were no Macs to design on in those days. But we did have border tape, glue sticks, and ideas. The rest was a matter of execution. I started by drawing a box, a perfect rectangle, then, using thin border tape, configuring the profile of a stylized eagle. From the start, I liked what was appearing on the page, but I was not telling anyone. Casually, I asked about the "history" of the existing eagle. Bodette, always gracious, enthusiastic, and ten steps ahead of me, had compiled the historic information: The eagle nameplate had survived two World Wars, the Korean War, and the Vietnam War, and it sat proudly there on July 20, 1969, when man first set foot on the moon. I could read between the lines as Bodette and I reviewed this over lunch one very cold day: "Mario, this eagle means history here." Yes, the eagle and St. Cloud readers had more than a mere casual relationship.

During lunch one day, I had decided to tell only Bodette about my idea to dethrone the eagle and replace it with a minimalist rectangle and a very thin-lined shape of an eagle inside. Always open to the next idea, Bodette did not seem to brush my idea aside instantly.

"Why don't we tell the others, Mario?" he asked me as he got ready to pay for our lunch and head back to the newsroom. Bodette knew his colleagues well, I must say. The publisher of the Times and many of his editors developed a normal case of cold feet when the discussion of the eagle took place.

"We are not getting rid of the eagle totally," I hurried to say. "It is just that we put in a more modern one."

Half the people in the room were at least curious; others stayed quiet and seemed confused but not at all convinced. I emerged from that long and mentally exhausting meeting with at least hesitant permission to try my rectangle with the stylized eagle inside. Upon my return to Syracuse, I knew I would have to generate something magnificent before sending it for review.

For many nights in a row, I sat at my drafting board (remember those?), watching the snow fall outside, while my nine-year-old son Mario Jr. stood by my side, doing his own drawings while I sketched, watching me maneuver around an X-ACTO knife. Some may not know what an X-ACTO knife is—call it a weapon of choice for artists and designers in the newsroom, seldom used for bad intentions.

Finally, I had the design, put it on a page, and placed type around it. Since this boxed eagle would not sit there alone, it had to work with the rest of the design. If nothing else, Mario Jr. and I were both fans.

NEW EAGLE LANDS IN ST. CLOUD.

Arriving in St. Cloud on another snowy day, I showed the prototype design to Bodette first, then Don Casey. They both liked it, Bodette more so, and he was already jumping with joy at the sight of this new, younger offspring of the old, tired, and ugly eagle.

But we had to convince a whole lot of other people, and eventually, we had to win over the Gannett execs, who were in Rochester, New York, at the time. In my correspondence, as I lobbied for my new eagle concept, I wrote the following: " . . . notice that I am proposing a radical change for the nameplate. But you will notice that your eagle has been preserved, if only in very abstract terms. Of course, I would not part with the eagle . . . I feel that we can reach this happy compromise—keeping it but minimizing its impact."

By 2010, the word "compromise" had become part of my consulting vocabulary, but little did I know at the time how much compromise would be the one tool I never left home without. Every presentation must have compromise. The consultant, editor, or art director who is not ready to compromise will perish along the way—or self-destruct.

Also, the phrase "keeping it but minimizing its impact" is one I have probably attached to almost all of my 500-plus projects at one point or another. That minimized American eagle of compromise taught me much in this first project, but its impact on my career would come later, after the paper was launched—yes, with the new stylized eagle.

WHAT THE READERS SAID.

The new eagle concept went to Gannett headquarters for final approval, and I knew it would not be an easy sell, but, hey, we had overcome all the obstacles locally in the St. Cloud newsroom, so how difficult could it be? When a newspaper is part of a group, the locals produce the paper, but the execs at headquarters decide in a few minutes what works or doesn't. This is not limited to the world of newspapers. In fact, it may be a widespread practice for the "hands on deck" people to keep the place going and know what works best but be subjected to the decisions, and often whims, of major players years removed from the day-to-day operations. Consultants need to establish good dialogue with those hands-on people who hold the keys—and very often solutions

–to move the project forward. More cold feet came when Rochester reported that the change was too drastic and might shock readers.

However, as Bodette reminded me in an email years later, in the end, headquarters advised adopting the new eagle in St. Cloud. I do not know why the big shots changed their mind. I was just elated that they did and have never questioned what the epiphany was. Were readers really shocked?

This is an argument that I still hear weekly in some newsrooms around the world. I've learned that most ideas shock editors and publishers but few shock readers. Readers tend to be open-minded to change almost everywhere! Put that on my headstone, please.

And while we're at it: Editors and publishers are more likely to be fearful, skeptical, and afraid of change! Somehow, the locals in St. Cloud had fallen in love with the stylized eagle, and the publisher managed to get a go-ahead. On March 17, 1980, the new eagle officially flew into the front page of the **St. Cloud Daily Times.** In the process, the old eagle took the article "The" from the logo as well–good riddance. Now, **St. Cloud Daily Times** was the name, and a boxed, stylized eagle was perched on the corner of the front page. A hush fell over the newsroom that first day, waiting for the forecast reader reaction.

What would they say? How many would cancel subscriptions because the old eagle had flown away forever? Hotlines were put into effect at the switchboard. Editors and reporters volunteered to staff the phones, all ready to persuade "furious" readers who would call, indignant about change, inflamed that their newspaper had modified its logo. To the surprise of the editors, few readers even noticed that the old eagle was gone, and even fewer missed it.

Given it was my first project, I had no idea what to expect. For the first time, I nervously wondered if I had committed some major crime against tradition, an unpatriotic act that could cause the government to revoke my citizenship and send me back to Cuba (horror of horrors). This could be my first and last project, I told myself. But then I was a professor, so maybe this project would allow me to teach students what not to do. As you may have anticipated, despite the preparation and bracing for the onslaught, nothing came of it. There was no reaction whatsoever, much to the surprise of the editors.

A team of marketing people set up calls in the evening of the first day of the redesign to survey subscribers and find out what they thought about the new look of the paper, with hints of "What do you think of the new logo?" Surprise. Not one negative call. And surprise number two, some of the subscribers asked: "What logo are you referring to?" Here was this eagle that had been sitting at the top of page one for decades, no longer there, and nobody noticed?

THE RESEARCH OF EAGLES, LOGOS, AND THE REST.
Instantly, the **St. Cloud Daily Times** eagle logo change was a cause célèbre in the industry. So much so that the American Newspaper Publishers Association commissioned a study of reader reaction to the change of logo in St. Cloud. (1) The results, published for all to see, revealed that the change of logo had not affected perception, consumption, or level of subscription and that, indeed, some readers were not even aware of the dramatic change.

When I said earlier that the eagle had long-haul wings, I mean it in terms of my own career. Work never stopped for me again. Not because this design was anything that set the world on fire but because the story of the eagle was told and retold. I still do seminars in the US, and inevitably, some older person in the audience will say, "You're the one who changed the St. Cloud eagle, right?"

"Yes, I did" is my usual, proud response—and then I thank serendipity and luck for putting that patriotic icon in front of me. Many years later, Bodette reminded me that before we even signed a contract, he and I were sitting at lunch at the American Press Institute in Reston, Virginia, and he showed me his newspaper and asked if I would be interested in working with them. Apparently, I responded by saying, "Yes, please, let's do it so I can get rid of that ugly eagle on your nameplate." Shame on me—not very diplomatic! St. Cloud was my first project redesigning a daily

66 *As consultants, we aim to spark transformative ideas or deliver insights in workshops that propel us to new heights in the marketing world. For me, the St. Cloud Daily Times eagle soared and so did my career."*

newspaper from start to finish. I had done dozens of weeklies around upstate New York but no dailies until then. Many lessons from St. Cloud shaped my style of work, my behavior with clients, and my belief in myself. The project confirmed the fact that we consultants sell and promote ideas. The best consultants believe in their ideas, present them clearly and enthusiastically, and promote them with passion and conviction. In that sense, the consultant can soar higher than any eagle—especially the old one in St. Cloud.

TAKE AIM
The First One Counts Extra

Your first consulting job may come about serendipitously, with luck and timing playing a role. More often, however, it happens because you've excelled in your full-time job—consistently providing innovative ideas, standing out to your team, and earning the respect of your bosses. Someone is likely to notice how you break away from the pack, and soon, an invitation arrives to share your expertise and enthusiasm beyond your current role. That becomes your first consulting project. From there, it's up to you to seize the moment and step confidently into the role of a consultant. Reflecting on what the St. Cloud project did for my consulting career, I often say I would have been wise to do it for free. So give that first project your best effort, put in the extra hours, and reap the rewards as you begin your journey as a consultant.

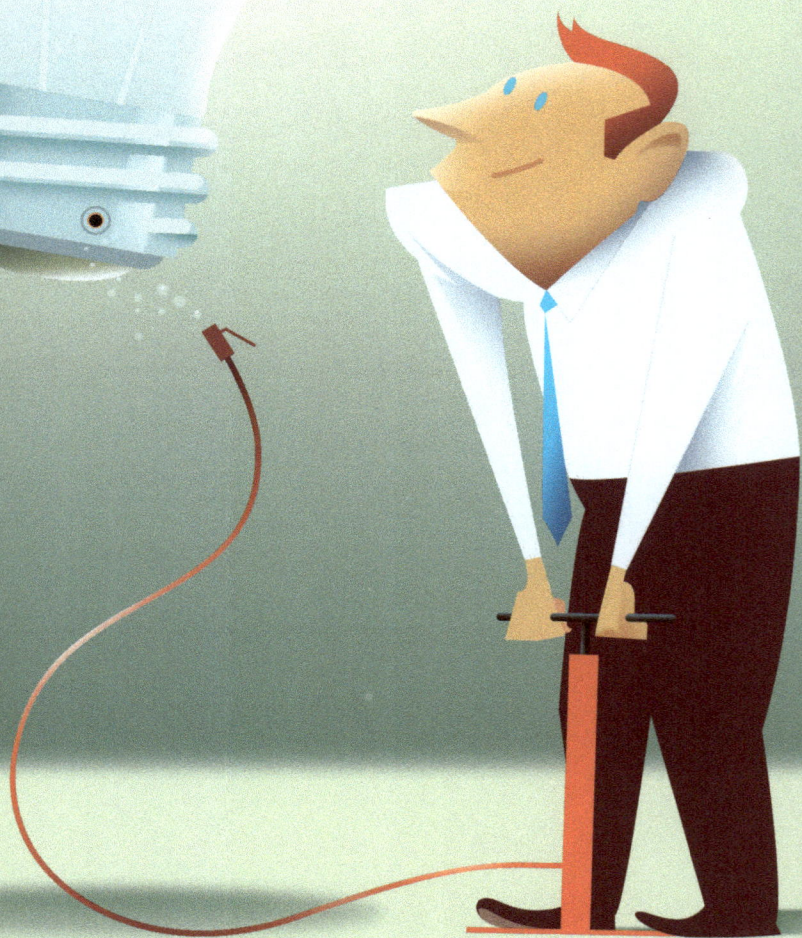

Characteristics of the Ideal Consultant

Taking a consulting project to successful completion requires the effort and talents of many. When all goes well, the in-house team assembled for the project when the consultant arrives is composed of the most talented people. Everyone in that project team has something unique to offer. The project leader understands the essential goals to be accomplished; plus, they bring a level of expertise on the subject.

Unfortunately, the project group we consultants face upon starting a project may not be ideal. Why? Some groups are inevitably put together with internal politics in mind. A person's talent and organizational abilities may be second to the fact that the supervisor CEO/decision-maker likes them. Sometimes a team is assembled on the basis of seniority. If someone has been sitting at a desk in the newsroom for twenty years, she will gain a spot in the most desirable project of the organization. Seniority often trumps ability. What is the consultant to do in such situations?

THE CONSULTANT BUILDS TEAMS (IDENTIFIES TALENT).
Part of a consultant's job is to identify talent, be honest about the make-up of the project group, and establish the necessary skills within the group. For example, I had a project to redesign the digital operation of a major daily newspaper, yet the project group of eleven members had seven editors with little knowledge of technology and even less familiarity with design. This requires diplomacy.

I presented the situation to the publisher. The response I was met with was something like, "Well, you know how it goes, Mario. These seven editors work together, and we simply could not leave any of them out of the project team. Hope you understand."

Of course I understood. However, I used our lunch break away from the office to outline for the publisher what a successful project team would look like and the need to include technical types from the IT department and design. By the time I was lifting my espresso mini tasse, the CEO was making a phone call. Presto, the wheels were in motion to recompose the project team. The situation had to be dealt with diplomatically, but I also could not push forward with the project group, not when 50 percent of the decisions were design-related, and especially given the high ratio of technology decisions that had to be made. Being a consultant has sometimes felt like being a traffic cop, standing at the intersection of journalism, technology, and design. The groups assigned to work on a project with me must have representatives from all. At times, identifying and locating leadership is also a main component of the consultant's job, even if it is not anywhere on the list of deliverables in the contract.

One time, I was working in the north of Argentina, with renowned regional newspaper **La Gaceta.** Brought in for a major redesign, I didn't have an art director to work with. Seasoned consultants know that they can usually create the perfect project. However, if the in-house team is not ready to execute it, success will be elusive. How could I deliver a design concept and put it in the hands of journalists with no interest and/or knowledge of the essentials of design, such as typography, color, and grid configurations?

Here I was, in a location where finding an art director would not be easy. So I decided to inquire about artists in any department of the newspaper, knowing that–especially in Latin America–one could often find tremendously talented artists in departments other than the newsroom. I was right. We found a young artist employed in the advertising department who spent his days drawing birthday cakes and balloons for birthday messages in the classified pages. After a brief conversation, he told me that he was a painter whose work was exhibited in local galleries. After I saw some of his work, he drew his last balloon that week. We moved him to the newsroom, and he began to put his artistic magic to work, with pages that eventually became major winners in all the international newspaper design contests.

Discovering talent. Assembling project groups. Defining roles within the project group. Moving people around. All these are part of the role that the consultant plays as an outside leader who comes into an organization to play the role of the human resources manager with a special mission: the success of the project.

Identifying talent is one of the most rewarding aspects of a consultant's work. Several times I have encountered a truly talented person in the newsroom–a gifted designer or a talented, seasoned editor. I would ask them, "How come you are not the art director? The managing editor?"

The answer was typically, "Well, I have been bypassed for promotion many times." The person in front of me could have been a leader in the team, and here they were, another body in the room. Worse than being fired is being kept in a job without recognition or promotion, prevented from seeking greener pastures for professional growth.

THE CONSULTANT IS A GUEST IN THE HOUSE.
My mantra about this issue is simple and to the point. When I enter a building where my services as a consultant have been required, I know that I am a guest in that house. It gives me a sense of boundaries to live by and helps me see my role more clearly. It helps me read the signals that I should simply retreat to another room.

Like guests in a home, consultants must respect the institutional privacy of the clients. When two or three managers begin to have an internal discussion that becomes heated in front of me, I do the same as a houseguest of a couple who starts arguing in the kitchen during breakfast. I say, "I think I will have my coffee by the river this morning, to enjoy nature a little bit." Everyone appreciates that, especially the people in the fight. Even when the clients in the heated discussion are doing so in a language that I do not understand, I follow body language and make my retreat pronto.

Respecting boundaries is not just about physical space but also about understanding the cultural and organizational norms of the client. Each organization has its unique dynamics, and as a consultant, it is crucial to navigate these with empathy and respect. This mindset ensures that I am always perceived as a respectful guest, which in turn enhances the effectiveness of my consultancy. This philosophy is a cornerstone of my approach to consulting, enabling me to build strong, respectful, and effective relationships with my clients.

THE CONSULTANT DEVELOPS TRUST.
An essential for a good consultant/client relationship is trustworthiness, which is cultivated through various behaviors and practices such as active listening to the client's needs and concerns; showing genuine empathy and concern for the client's situation; being transparent about intentions, capabilities, and limitations; and maintaining reliable performance and communication. In their book *The Trusted Advisor*, authors David Maister, Charles Green, and Robert Galford emphasize the importance of building trust and relationships with clients. A key point: understanding the client's perspective—that is, seeing the world through the client's eyes. (1)

Margarita Moreno, who had a twenty-year career as an international tax consultant (mostly at Ernst & Young), uses the term "trusted advisor" to describe effective consultants: *"In the legal business, we also have the role of 'trusted advisor'—it's like a pseudo consultant. As an international tax attorney, my consulting was really as a subject matter expert. Especially when I was at a law firm (Fulbright & Jaworski, now Norton Rose Fulbright) and at Ernst & Young, I was hired*

❝ You can never predict which project will amplify your expertise the most. I've learned that sometimes, the most unassuming endeavors capture the greatest spotlight."

because of my tax technical expertise. In my experience though, the relationship I built with my clients is what allowed my role to go from subject matter expert to consultant and 'trusted advisor' where the consulting really grew outside of my subject matter expertise . . . It's a leap of faith for the businesses to trust a consultant. As a result, building trust, building relationships is crucial." (2)

THE CONSULTANT OFFERS ADVICE, PRESENTS OPTIONS, AND ENHANCES THE DIALOGUE.

As a consultant, you have been invited to offer advice, present ideas, and share your experiences in similar projects, but the discussion belongs to the people who own the project, not to the consultant. As such, it has always helped me to appear willing to follow the program planned for me by those closest to the project. Rather than arrive with agendas, I offer agendas only if a request for such appears.

The successful consultant lets the in-house project leader run the show and have ownership of the project. Your role as a consultant is to become the project leader's ally to the point where, by the middle of the project, you are seen as a duo, both contributing to the project's success.

When the consultant dominates every discussion, acts with a know-it-all attitude, and talks more than he listens, usually the people in the room are turned off, and, consequently, the project fails to reach its potential. Consultants should be catalysts who facilitate change rather than impose solutions. By enabling clients to find their own solutions and empowering them to implement changes, consultants create lasting impact. Let the client feel ownership of the project.

THE CONSULTANT IS A PARTNER IN A LEARNING PROCESS, NOT SOMEONE WHO IMPOSES IDEAS.

Those who work with me (especially my team at **García Media**) know this rule: The best idea wins, regardless of where it came from. When I work as a consultant, I first impress upon those inside the organization that we will have a "Sunday brunch of ideas" during our discussions, and how the best idea will win. If a project is full of good ideas, everyone wins. So, whether we are conducting a briefing at the start of a project, sketching pages or screens, prototyping a zero number, or getting ready for the introductory marketing campaign, we sit at a table and let every idea land there, like confetti from a huge piñata.

The confident consultant is comfortable with abandoning his own ideas quickly when presented with a superior idea. Margarita Moreno has also spoken about her belief in collaboration between consultant and in-house teams. "Collaboration is a concept that is sometimes missing and has been the key to my success in my career. Too many consultants come in as 'experts' (which they usually are) and fail to collaborate with their clients. The worst consultants are those who already have the answer before even entering the room!" (3)

PERSONAL NOTE
Building on Ideas of the In-House Team

Moreno feels that consultants are great sounding boards for raw ideas. "The best consultants bring a different perspective from that of their clients and are able to enhance raw ideas by bringing that perspective to life. They are able to build on ideas and are not necessarily tied to presenting their own ideas." (4)

Or, as I often tell my teams, "Let the best idea win," especially when the organization has talented individuals with niche expertise. Make them your partners. Working together, good things happen. I always want to be surrounded by people who have more talent, experience, and ingenuity than me.

When we combine forces, good things happen. The project soars. Everybody wins. When my own art directors at **García Media** start sketching a project, I usually start with my own sketches—not because I want to impose them, but because I'm the chief architect of the project. By assimilating briefings thoroughly, I want to make sure that those first scribbles on paper or screen (we call it Version A) carry the essence of what the clients have said they want.

However, I usually tell my designers, "Whatever you do, please complete a version of my sketch, then go ahead and do whatever other versions of my sketches and briefing you are inspired to do." The results of more than 560 projects to date are amazingly different styles and divergent ideas that come together to form a unified visual statement. There is no repetition or monotony in what we do, because, although the process is similar (a proven methodology that works each time in terms of systematic work), the creative part is totally different, allowing serendipity to be ever present in my toolbox.

While doing the redesign of **The Journal** in 2001, we often walked around the World Trade Center, in Lower Manhattan, during lunch hour. It was summertime, and everyone stepped out from **The Journal** offices to enjoy a bit of lunch in the sunshine. Every day, we would hear the same music playing from the same grinding organ by the same little old man, who, complete with his cart and organ, carried the necessary monkey to add to the entertainment.

If you gave the monkey a quarter, the music would start, again and again. Obviously, and I am sure many people think so, a consultant could be like the monkey and the organ grinder in the park. Give me a quarter and I play the same song, again and again. Never forget this: Those paying for the services of a consultant don't want sameness and repetition. They want you to bring a body of work and experience to utilize as you face the specific challenges and problems of one very special client who hired you.

Each presentation I do is expressly for that specific client. The same was true in my years as a professor. Every three years or so, I would do the summer ritual of emptying all my files of handouts, lectures, slides, etc.; fill plastic bags with the stuff; and, without thinking twice, put it all in the trash.

Come the fall semester, I would pretend I was a new teacher, presenting the course for the first time. Hard work, indeed, but a sense of renewal came with it. Consultants should do the same in their work. Recycling is good for the environment but quite lethal for the consultant. No two businesses are alike. Amen. No two project leaders resemble each other•

THE CONSULTANT MUST ADAPT.

As a child actor, I learned that we could be doing the same play five times a week. In the theater, actors adapt to the audience. We could be doing the same play five times a week, but each night, the audience would react differently to a joke or a bit of business.

That is why we adapted the performance to the audience. Boring audiences usually drew boring performances. The same strategy of adaptability applies to effective consultancy.

In fifty-five years, I have consulted for over 750 organizations in 122 countries to date. But it was just after project number forty that I already knew this one idea: The stuff that played with gusto in Buenos Aires was not going to get you anywhere in Hamburg, Istanbul, or Bucharest! It is much better, healthier, more challenging, and, indeed, more fun to put a blank canvas in front of you that first day you enter the building where a new project awaits. Even after many years, you will still find the work thrilling–that feeling of not knowing what you will find.

PERSONAL NOTE
Pretend You're Part of the Team

A great consultant needs to be a great actor. That is, they must pretend they are part of the team that will have to live with the changes being made. They must pretend to work full time at the organization. And most importantly, they must never mix one project with the other.

In my career, sometimes I have worked in four countries in just seven days. While my body moves, I follow certain routines. One of those is that when I land in a new city to consult on one project, I make myself believe that I work there full time, that this is a team I am part of, and that I don't remember the project I left twelve hours ago. Also, I have to block out the project I'm headed to in three days. Part of this ritual is settling in the hotel room like it is home: I unpack my suitcase and hang my clothes, and I often go out and buy fresh flowers to make the ambience more homelike and cheerful. If the engagement involves a weekend stay, I will head out to the local supermarket and stock up on fruit and yogurts. In the process, I get to meet local folks and engage in conversation, such as "Where do you get the news from most of the time?"

If I were to mix projects, cities, countries, and cultures, I would not be here still. The clients know this, and they appreciate it. Whoever I am with, this practice has the added benefit of them experiencing my total and full attention. There is a Zen-like approach to staying hyperpresent. For the consultant working across the globe, a clear understanding of culture is key to the success of the project. An example specific to my type of consulting with media—but applicable to many other fields—is that of selecting a color palette for a newspaper's website. When the project is in one of the Scandinavian countries, the color palette is composed of soft hues. Consultants observe the world around them. Notice that curtains in most Scandinavian homes are plain white. Thus, the color palette of the newspaper will reflect this. If, however, the project is in São Paulo, Brazil, where the consultant can see curtains in green, yellow, and red, the newspaper should reflect those color choices. It's called "adaptability," the art of contributing universal themes to help with reorganization of a company, but with a keen eye on the culture in which it thrives. Part of being involved as a full-timer means knowing the people more intimately. I get to know the secretaries, the assistants, the ones who make the coffee, and then, of course, the decision-makers/leaders. In practicing this approach, I have even visited some clients at home, spent time with their families. Long after the projects are finished, those relationships persist. I often fantasize that I could be stranded in hundreds of cities in over ninety countries and find a place to have a meal and a bed in someone's house. Of course, I arrived in all those places as a consultant, a total stranger, but today they would greet me as a friend. A perfect transformation is when the term *consultant* evolves into the word *friend* •

THE CONSULTANT IS A CHANGE AGENT.

When the consultant is hired, someone in the organization is thinking about change—or, more specifically, a strong need for change. Not everyone in the team may share that opinion, however. One can't over-emphasize the role of consultant as change agent. Change is what all humans instinctively avoid.

One of our former clients described his own experience with our consulting by saying, "You're the chaperone of change, ushering people to new places and making them do what they'll resist. It's an amazing service, requiring outsized talent."

Change is a formidable force, one that humans instinctively resist, clinging to the familiar and shunning the unknown. You'll see people clinging to the teddy bears of legacy, the way we have always done it. Yet, in the modern landscape of business, change is not merely inevitable, it is essential for survival and growth. As consultants, we step into this role with a profound sense of responsibility, guiding our clients through the tumultuous waters of transformation.

Our mission is clear: We are the chaperones of change. Our clients look to us not just for solutions but for the courage to embrace the new and different. Clients have nightmares of what they're afraid will happen. Consultants have to replace those with the dream and bring the dream to reality. Being a change agent demands a unique blend of skills such as a deep understanding of human psychology, an ability to communicate effectively, and an unwavering commitment to the client's goals.

We must listen intently, analyze astutely, and then act decisively. Our role is never to impose change but to facilitate it, making the journey as seamless and positive as possible.

THE CONSULTANT AS VALIDATOR.
A key role of the consultant is a validator—confirming what some in the internal project group already believe. As a former client wrote me: "In my experience, among your key roles was confirming and validating what I personally believed . . . . Contributing to the strength of convictions is super valuable. There's NO WAY I could have sold our project (and all that it meant and means) to that disparate group of publishers without the outside voice and evangelical validation of you—literally in the room. Hearing me, then hearing you in depth, with the CEO's quiet but tacit backing—irresistible, irrefutable."

One of the most critical and perhaps underappreciated functions of a consultant is that of validator. As consultants, we often find that many of the ideas and strategies we bring to the table are not entirely novel to the internal team. In fact, these concepts frequently reflect the thoughts and beliefs already held by key members of the organization.

Yet the power of our message is amplified precisely because it comes from an external source. "When you say it, it carries a lot of weight," another client once told me. "Remember, you are a taxi with the meter running, and the bosses are going to listen to you." This validation can transform tentative ideas into actionable strategies, fostering a sense of conviction and unity within the team.

Throughout my career, I have observed time and again how the presence and endorsement of an external consultant can solidify and elevate the internal dialogue. When we, as consultants, articulate and support the very ideas that internal team members have been advocating for, our endorsement serves as a powerful catalyst. It provides a sense of legitimacy and external credibility that can be pivotal in driving change and securing buy-in from broader stakeholders. Consider the implementation of Pinstripe, a project that involved a diverse group of publishers with varying priorities and perspectives. Internally, there were already champions of the project who believed in its potential and value. However, the path from belief to implementation required more than internal advocacy–it needed the authoritative voice of an external consultant. My role was not just to present new ideas but to echo and amplify the existing convictions within the organization.

Here, the usual challenges of a project had to be multiplied times forty, the number of different weekly business journals published in as many US cities, each newspaper with a different publisher and editor, and forty diverse views of what a weekly business newspaper should be like. In some cases, the publishers were quite happy with the way their product existed and were not too eager for a transformation that would give all forty titles the same design.

Selling an idea requires passion and a compelling narrative. In this case, my validation of the project, the enthusiasm and expertise of the project leader, and the CEO's quiet but unequivocal support created an irrefutable momentum. The internal team, already predisposed to the project's merits, found their own beliefs strengthened and their resolve fortified by an external voice that mirrored their own convictions.

In essence, the consultant's role as a validator is about more than just agreeing with internal ideas–it's about giving those ideas the weight and credibility they need to gain traction. This validation process is invaluable, as it helps align the organization, rallying disparate voices around a shared vision. Ultimately, the strength of conviction that a consultant brings to a project is one of the most valuable contributions we can make. By validating and reinforcing the ideas and beliefs already present within the organization, we help create a unified front, ready to tackle the challenges ahead with confidence and determination. It is a testament to the power of external validation and the critical role we play in facilitating and accelerating organizational change.

CONSULTANTS WHO DO LUNCH.
Nowhere is the consultant's role as confidant and father confessor more pronounced than during those lunches with members of the project team. It's difficult to remember a project without a dozen dramatic confessional lunches. It is part of the consultant's job.

I have sat through many, and while the setting varies, the sagas that are transacted over chicken salads and a glass of champagne are similar. Normally the person who puts lunch on the agenda has an agenda of his own. You are always one of a group of three: The one organizing the lunch brings an internal ally. Two for tea; two for good alliances. One speaks and whines, the friend validates and eats.

The consultant picks at her salad and listens to both sides, knowing that tomorrow, the next group comes in with a different story—and you pray that the venue will change, so at least the menu will be different. These lunches can be full of tension, occasionally tears. By the time coffee arrives, someone is pleading with you to "do something, since they listen to you." Be empathetic without meddling.

Occasionally, the person complaining has a rightful grievance. As the consultant, you listen, evaluate, become aware of the other side of the story, and proceed to advise supervisors accordingly. It is not all as it appears. Even people in high positions can be victims of superiors who try to block the person's idea at every turn. The ethical consultant is an objective observer who can, indeed, effect change and call attention to unfair situations within the management team.

A tip for these drama-infused lunches: Eat lightly, consume your full glass of bubbles, listen to all, make no promises. And remember, just like there are at least three ways to serve a caprese salad, there are usually more versions of the story waiting to be served.

As I became more experienced as a consultant, I emphasized that lunches are part of the workday, but I have opted for dinners by myself. Adding dinners with the clients to your agenda extends your day. And it is not a fun dinner, when the clients ask questions about the project and eat while you must choose whether to speak to answer questions or eat your meal. So I settled on this plan: yes to lunches, no to dinners.

ACCENTUATE THE POSITIVE.

Consultant alert: A positive attitude is the best of daily vitamins. Vitamin P has carried me through many situations where nothing in my surroundings was positive. In those moments, I reminded myself to be positive. The consultant's personal awareness plays a key role here.

Are you naturally positive or pessimistic? No doubt that plays a major role in your own perceptions and how hard you must work to remain positive. In every group, there will be at least one person who sees gloom, and nobody is going to convince this person that the sky isn't falling. It is part of group dynamics, happening at all levels, from family discussions to project deliberations.

One gloomy character in the mix I can usually handle, but have you ever been involved in a project where the saying "misery loves company" becomes reality? When two or more participants drag you and the project down? Stay alert and do not take sides.

Often, I have thought that project groups should be assembled following certain criteria, the most important of which is that everyone in this group must be open-minded, forward-thinking, and positive. That, of course, is wishful thinking on my part.

Try to see the bright side, and don't let the negative vibes within a group derail you or the project. Don't pay attention to those who see giant defeats where you see those little victories.

This, too, is part of what the consultant brings to the project group. A positive attitude is a vital tool for any consultant. It not only sustains your own motivation but also has the potential to uplift the entire project group. By focusing on the positives and refusing to be swayed by negativity, consultants can guide their clients toward achieving their goals and realizing their dreams.

GREAT IDEA
Effective Consultants Are Change Agents

Successful consultants:
- Build teams.
- Always remember that they are guests in the house where they are offering their services.
- Facilitate and offer advice.
- Enhance the internal dialogue.
- Validate the transformational beliefs already existing within the organization.
- Become partners in the learning process.
- Always think and act as if they are part of the internal project team.

Remember, you are an agent of change.

When All the Elements Click in a Project

My job as a consultant on a project is to ensure that the clients simply put on colorful wings; take off for unknown destinations; stop to explore an idea here, another there; and linger upon those that offer the best possibilities.

It is every consultant's dream project: You arrive, you do your basic reconnaissance, and you see possibilities for real innovation and transformation. Happens often. What does not happen so frequently is when the team heading your project—including the CEO—embraces your ideas readily. Such was the case with **El Tiempo**, Colombia's leading daily newspaper.

LET THE CLIENT SOAR.

This is how it all began. On a morning in October 2009, I arrived in Bogotá to start what would be my fourth redesign of **El Tiempo**, the dean of Colombian newspapers and one of the most respected in Latin America.

I had two cups of that wonderful Colombian coffee—two *tintos*, as the locals call the little demitasses with the robust brew of Juan Valdez's best. The art director, Beiman Pinilla, with whom I had worked on every single one of those redesigns, put seven days of **El Tiempo** on a table in front of me. That was it. That was all I needed to see to tell myself, *Mario, you don't want to redesign this newspaper one* *more time. Been there, done that. It really looks good. We just did it five years ago; why change it?* Sitting in front of the pile of newspapers, I remained quiet and then said: "You know, guys. I don't want to redesign **El Tiempo**, but it would be wonderful if we could pretend that this newspaper does not exist, and that we have assembled here today to create a new newspaper for Colombia—a modern newspaper that would have to survive in a multi-platform world!"

My declaration stunned the three or four designers around me, including our own **García Media** senior design director, Rodrigo Fino. Utter silence. There was not one response from anyone in that room, although I can only imagine what they were thinking.

NEXT STEP: TELLING THE CEO.
Within minutes, I decided to go see Luis Fernando Santos, the CEO of **El Tiempo** at the time. He welcomed me in his spacious office overlooking a vibrant green patch of the beautiful city of Bogotá. Another *tinto* later, I launched into my narrative: "Luis Fernando, I have always enjoyed working with **El Tiempo.** It is like family here.

"I think the paper looks nice as it is. But I also think it has too many sections, too deeply rooted in the content flow of a newspaper of another era. Perhaps we could step into the sandbox and pretend that you brought me here to create a new, nonexistent newspaper for 2011 and beyond. Start from scratch. New ideas, new concepts . . . " The visionary Luis Fernando looked at me, smiled (not at all surprised, I guess), and then said, "Go ahead, Mario. I don't promise you we will go all the way, but you and the team create how you envision this newspaper." It was one of those what-if? moments where the person in charge said, "Why not?"

The new **El Tiempo** was born. Going through all seven days of **El Tiempo,** I sketched the flow of how pages would go in the newspaper. Thinking like a reader, I decided on three daily sections: What you must know. What you must read. What you must do. In Spanish: *Debes Saber. Debes Leer. Debes Hacer.* Every bit of content that we put into a newspaper fits into one of those areas. But here was the catch: We would no longer have most of the sections of the newspaper as we knew them.

HOY, EN LA WEB

Video
Carlos 'Pibe' Valderrama, en entrevista exclusiva para nuestro portal de eltiempo.com

Galería interactiva
India celebra por lo alto la versión XIX de los Juegos de la Mancomunidad.

ÍNDICE

wall street
bogotá
breve
deportes
perfil
libro
rincón
columnas
hechos
sociales
panorámico
clasificados
judiciales

Vargas Llosa, un Nobel muy esperado

Cuando ya se sentía olvidado por la Academia Sueca, el escritor peruano **fue galardonado con el premio mayor** de la literatura.

Júbilo en América Latina por la noticia.

UNA PLUMA EXCEPCIONAL, PERO UN MAL CANDIDATO
El escritor y periodista Plinio Apuleyo Mendoza describe a su amigo.

EL PRIMER CAPÍTULO DE SU MÁS RECIENTE NOVELA
En el 'Sueño del celta' revive la historia de un diplomático irlandés.

REVALUACIÓN

El dólar más bajo en 2 años

El precio del dólar descendió ayer a 1.787 pesos, el nivel más bajo de los últimos dos años. Para frenar la revaluación, el Gobierno prepara medidas adicionales a la compra de divisas que está haciendo el Banco de la República. Una idea es buscar mecanismos para que las empresas que tienen que hacer pagos en el exterior no los conviertan a pesos y los sigan haciendo afuera.

Moneda de EE. UU., en descenso
Fuente: Banco de la República

2017,88
1786,20
21-may-10 · 08-Oct-10

Editorial

El Nobel a Vargas Llosa

El premio de la Academia Sueca no solo reconoce a un excelente narrador, sino también a quien ha hecho del oficio de escribir una pasión ética.

SE ESPERAN 4,5 MILLONES DE PARTICIPANTES

Hoy habrá simulacro de evacuación en Bogotá

Las 11 de la mañana de hoy es la hora fijada para que 4,5 millones de habitantes de Bogotá dejen de hacer lo que estén haciendo, busquen la salida más segura del sitio en el que estén y vayan a un punto de encuentro.

Así de sencillo y sin sirenas de alerta será el simulacro de evacuación que hará la ciudad para prepararse en caso de terremoto.

Trabajadores de 3.000 empresas y estudiantes de 120 colegios públicos y privados estarán entre los participantes.

FÚTBOL

'BOLILLO' QUIERE GANARLE A ECUADOR

En el sexto partido de la era Hernán D. Gómez, Colombia enfrenta hoy al equipo de Rueda en el Red Bull Arena, de Nueva York. T.V. a las 7:30 p.m.

POR CRECIMIENTO DE 'MOTOTAXISMO'

Les ponen pico y placa a motos en Bucaramanga

Desde el próximo lunes, la capital santandereana restringirá la libre circulación de motocicletas como medida para controlar el creciente fenómeno del 'mototaxismo'. El pico y placa se hará efectivo entre las 6 y las 8 a.m. y las 5 y las 8 p.m., de lunes a viernes, y funcionará de acuerdo con el último dígito del vehículo. Medida similar han adoptado Barranquilla y Medellín.

Ayer, representantes de los motociclistas anunciaron protestas por considerar injusta la medida.

This is the front page of El Tiempo after the major transformation of content organization.

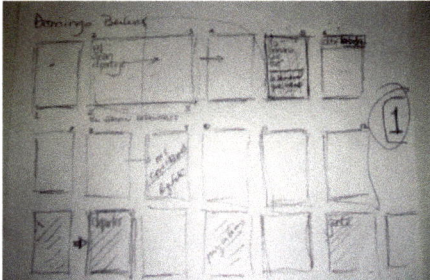

Here is my first sketch for sequencing how the different topics would appear, an exercise in information architecture.

This is what the team had produced by the end of that one day of creating the concept. We had no idea about the color coding, nothing more than just content sectioning.

Sequencing was followed by sketches of how the three major "books" would look.

Without wasting any time, the team got to create section headers to describe what you Must Know, Must Read, Must Do.

DEBES SABER (WHAT YOU MUST KNOW).

Debes Saber (what you must know) would be the first section, the one part of the newspaper you would read with your morning coffee. Text's not too long, but comprehensive enough. We assigned a color to this section–blue.

The opening section of *Debes Saber*: blue, active, combines Bogotá, Nation, World, Business, and Politics. Also Sports (*Deportes*) appears here.

DEBES LEER (WHAT YOU MUST READ)

The in-depth section covers opinion, analysis, and interpretation, along with columnists. Sometimes a story that merits four paragraphs in *Debes Saber* gets a full analysis in *Debes Leer*. This section is green to signal to the reader that this content is going to be the more leisurely read of the day. Green indicates meditative reading, so they may opt to read *Debes Leer* during a lunch break or in the evening.

Debes Leer is the living room, where you kick off your shoes and lie down to read your favorite column, editorial, or in-depth report, without a care in the world.

The opening section of Debes Leer (what you must read), green color and indicates more in depth material.

DEBES HACER (WHAT YOU MUST DO)

Debes Hacer is all about activity. The color orange invites you to move, to get out of the house, go for a jog, walk your dog, go shopping for a new computer, or get tips on how to take a vacation with the kids or a romantic getaway with your partner. This was a fun and easy one to plan: Health, fitness, relationships, food, wine, beauty, fashion—it all fits here. *Debes Hacer* is the outdoors, or the home gym, or the swimming pool area.

Debes Hacer (What you must do) is all about Lifestyle, health, Fitness and things to do.

SPORTS IS PART OF *DEBES SABER* (WHAT YOU MUST KNOW).

For obvious reasons, "Sports" (Deportes) continues to be a self-contained section, but it appears under the *Debes Saber* blue section. After much discussion, the project group decided that sports had to remain its own section.

Sports pages retain their traditional identity.

USING BLUE LABELS.

In the reorganization of content at **El Tiempo**, (1) it is possible for a business story to appear next to a city police story. Indeed, these are strange bedfellows, so blue labels are used to indicate subject matter.

The labels are not intrusive and simply say "Bogotá," "Business," "World," etc. This was an idea our **García Media** team suggested and was embraced by the editorial team and then presented to their superiors.

Editors who thought the lack of traditional headers for content would hit readers the wrong way were very happily surprised with the results. During focus groups, readers liked the labels and had no trouble whatsoever reading the stories without confusion. In fact, I must say that the focus groups for this project, which involved 600 readers and nonreaders throughout major cities in Colombia, must rank among the most thorough—and represented the most satisfying results in my career.

Notice the blue labels (under circles), which in this page mix stories about the Nation, Justice, Sports and the World.

◎ | TAKE AIM
Keep Your Eyes Open for Potential

Often, when everything clicks in a project, it's the consultant's hand that has made it happen. You arrive at the start, meet the team, and quickly sense that this group is unusually enthusiastic and open to new ideas. That's your signal that this project has the potential to go beyond easy solutions and quick fixes. This was the case with **El Tiempo**, where my team and I recognized a significant opportunity for experimentation. While this scenario doesn't occur every time, it happens often enough that it's up to the consultant to seize the moment—dream big and guide the client on an adventure of innovation and experimentation. This approach usually leads to strong results, creating a success story that not only enhances the consultant's reputation but also paves the way for future opportunities.

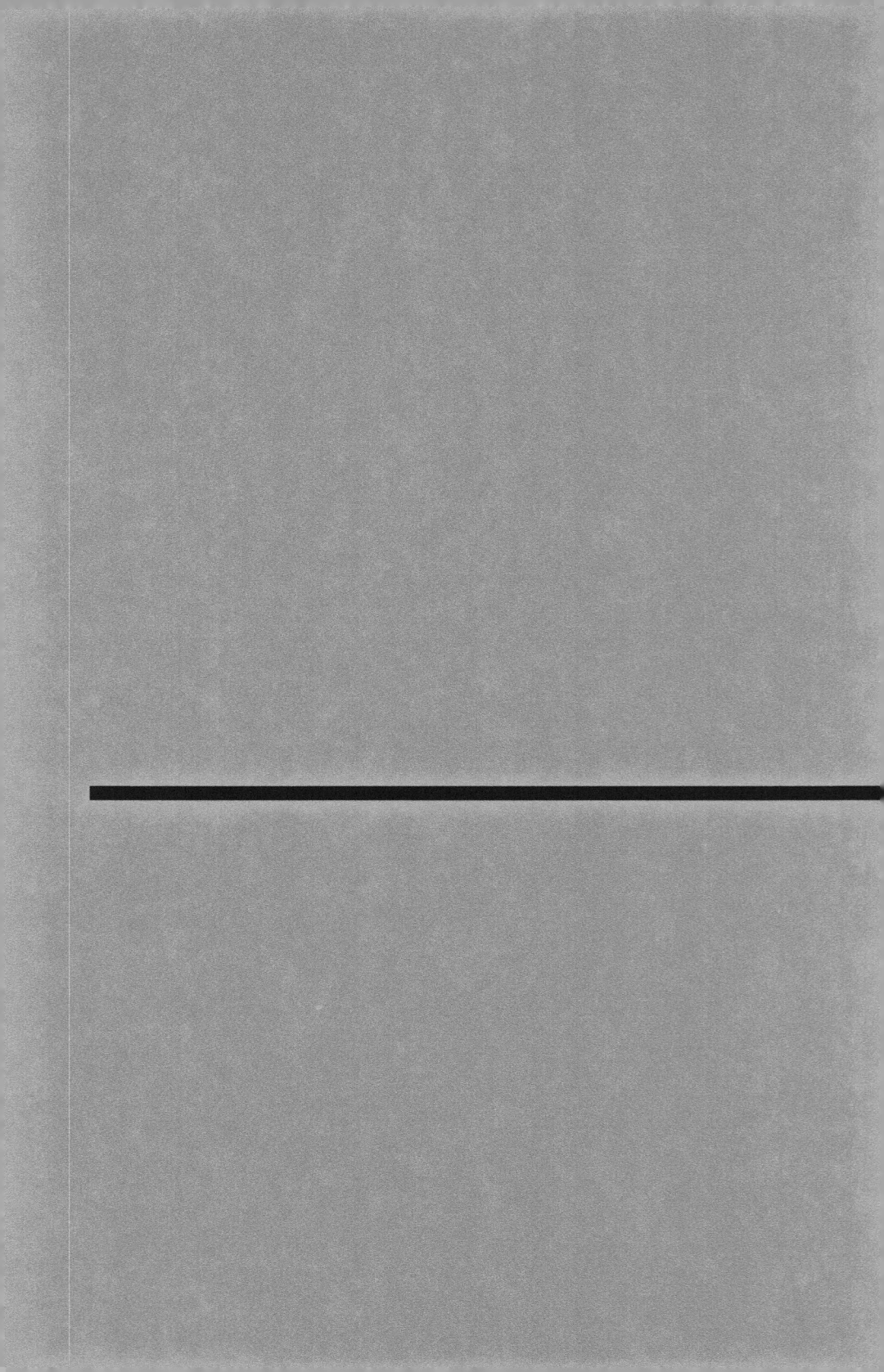

The Basics

Part 2

Respect Traditions

One time, I had a meeting in Germany at a company with a rather strict, formal approach to business. A member of my team embarrassed me, although he was totally unaware that he was doing so. We were in the CEO's suite, with a fabulous view of the city's skyline. The CEO's assistant walked in with a silver tray full of gorgeous glasses and bottles of mineral water. My team member proceeded to grab a bottle, opened it, and drank directly from the bottle. This was not an afternoon with the guys at the local bowling alley. The CEO looked at him, as did the assistant, and I could see a red flashing sign that read "ugly American" in their heads. Nothing prepares you for such episodes. Indeed, you don't know what you don't know. On the positive side, the consultant learns the lesson when these situations pop up, analyzes what went wrong, and consider show to avoid the same problem in the future.

As I read the literature of guides to consulting, I see various references to a consultant's systematic approach to tackling a project, or a general model of consulting. If there is a general model of the consulting process—a step-by-step framework that outlines the consulting process from start to finish—I did not have that at the start of my consulting career. It was more like learning by doing.

However, by staying open-minded and learning with every project, my team and I have developed some essentials that we apply successfully to our projects, recognizing that each project is unique. Because we work globally, we must be aware not only of the in-house culture of a certain media company but also the country's traditions and ways of approaching life and work.

Clients vary in the way business is conducted in their organizations. Some clients require that executives dress in a business casual style, and especially more mature clients expect mature consulting behavior. The consultant must adapt to the client's expectations as much as possible. As for the person on my team drinking straight from the bottle of water, I had a short chat with him. It never happened again.

Here are the four steps that we follow with each project (and will get into in more detail in the next section):

1. Briefing
2. Sketching
3. Prototyping
4. Implementation

Whatever area of expertise the consultant deals with, create a template of how you approach the project to provide continuity and to facilitate the creation of timelines to give the project a focus and sense of order.

Learning to Be a Consultant

A major motivator for writing this book is to provide the kind of preparation that I lacked myself when I became a consultant. I don't know of any graduate degrees in consulting or even courses that offer step-by-step instructions for the art, craft, and reality of consulting. I did not have a guide to consulting at the start of my career, and now, five decades later, I still face daily challenges when a situation arises that has never appeared before and demands action.

Like many others, I landed in the role of consultant without much previous preparation. I simply was doing my work as best as I could, and people noticed, then they wanted me to share my experience and knowledge. In the baptism-by-fire rituals that have been such a part of my professional life, I immediately learned a few lessons that have served me well all along while acting as a consultant.

With each new project comes major new learning for the consultant. It took years and many flights between cities and continents to get down several of these lessons: Act as if you are a guest in the house where you are consulting; offer advice and present options, but do not dominate the dialogue; become a good listener and partner in the learning process, not one who imposes ideas; treat each project as if it were your first; and emphasize the uniqueness of each project.

📎 SAVE IT
Be Nice. Be Understanding. But Be Firm

Navigating the human condition inside an organization requires skills that no class can ever prepare you for. Indeed, you are always the guest in the house. At the same time, everyone in the organization looks up to you as the expert who is bringing new information and transformation to whatever craft is practiced in the house. You command respect. You are expected to know it all, display empathy, avoid favoritism to anyone in the team, and be a good listener. Remember, the effective consultant is aware of the importance of interpersonal relationships.

___

THE PITCH.

Consultants must become experts at the pitch. This is the audition, your chance to strut your stuff and convince people in power at a certain organization that you are worth their time and money. It is your chance to convince the client that they can trust you.

Clients want to partner with trustworthy consultancies. In fact, 87 percent of clients say that trust is more important for their purchasing decisions in consulting services since COVID, according to a consulting overview by **Source Global Research.** [1]

Potential clients want to know who they're buying from. They want to know what you do, what you specialize in, how you approach your client work, and why they should do business with you. Clients tend to stay with their current consulting firms if those companies have proven themselves as trusted advisors already. In my own work, I can testify to this, as more than 60 percent of my consulting work is with returning clients. About 50 percent of my clients come from referrals.

Today's pitch may be more competitive and will require that you prove your expertise in more detail than even five years ago. To me, the pitch is part of the excitement of competing. And the US is the land of opportunity, but also the capital of competition.

I learned that early upon landing in the US as a refugee, thanks to my Uncle Kiko. He was our own Mambo King–Hector García, the barber–or *Tio Kiko*, as we in the family referred to him. A colorful man with colorful shirts and a master of the trumpet, with which he played songs of love.

"It is all about competition in this country," Tio Kiko told me on my second day in the United States, back in 1962. Then he added, "This is the place where you compete for everything, and if you are good, you make it." You see, though *Tio Kiko* was a barber by day, he played a mean trumpet by night in the Miami Beach nightclubs of another era. This is America, the land where competition thrives and the best person wins. Tio Kiko had it right. I have remembered his words at every pitch—more times than I can count. But with each pitch comes anxiety, fear, the nervous stomach the night before, with little sleep, and, of course, that big red sign we all hate to see in front of our faces: rejection. Yet a consultant pitching projects must learn to accept rejection. The best person wins. Tio Kiko had it right.

WHEN REJECTION STINGS.
Consultants enter the room to pitch their services full of energy, enthusiasm, and, of course, a positive attitude. "This is our project to win" is a phrase that has echoed in my head like the refrain in a good Edgar Allan Poe piece. So when the consultant gives that presentation, the best she has to offer, emphasizing that there is no other consultant who could solve this client's problems or interpret their dreams better, but the response is lukewarm, the consultant feels deflated. It's happened to all of us. Before the official news arrives that you have not been chosen for the project, you already sensed it when you left the presentation.

If a presentation is successful, the signs are usually there to provide the consultant with a sense of success—of continuity for this project with this client. If this was a morning presentation, there is an invitation for lunch with the principal stakeholders. Afternoon presentations lead to happy hour for further discussion. When a presentation goes well, the clients want to extend the presentation, moving it to more personal exchanges and "getting to know you" sessions. Next, there is a question of availability and even discussions of timelines. When the project leader asks, "How soon can we start?" that is a sign that you have succeeded in convincing the client that you are the essential consultant for the project. Don't be shy to ask your prospective clients how many other potential consultants are being considered. This is helpful to know where you stand, especially if you can get a sense of who the competition might be.

After every rejection, I make it a point to devote twenty-four hours to thinking about the possible reasons for not getting that specific job. The lessons of rejections stay with you —and just like when you land the job, you need to analyze what worked and what might have worked better. When you don't land it, it's arguably even more important to allow time to process and assess to better prepare you for the next pitch. It must be part of the human condition that good follow-up experiences become part of the normal, but oh, those rejections sting, and we spend more time meditating on them, so I have more details to offer you about various rejections.

One specifically still stings, thirty-eight years later. I failed to prepare properly for that specific client, a major newspaper title in New England. I should have arrived with images of where this newspaper's design failed and offered a couple of examples of how I could fix it. I learned later that the consultant who won the gig did so. Lesson learned: Make a case for why the client needs your expertise.

Another rejection moment, this time for a European title who I would still love to get my hands on today, taught me that I should have learned more about the background of the very conservative members of the board, all of whom were against using color. There I was, showing how this title would look with deep blue for its iconic logo. Lesson learned: It's good to know who is going to be judging your presentation, then tailor your comments accordingly. (Note: That title continues to be black and white, and the iconic logo is not likely to turn blue or red in my lifetime. The one that got away.)

Make rejection moments the consultant's graduate school. Analyze what went wrong, and be aware of situations where rejection has nothing to do with what you did but with the fact that, while there was a pitch process, the main stakeholders had already decided whom they wished to hire. Don't let rejection weigh you down. Instead, take the lessons learned and apply them to your next pitch. Often, failure comes down to a single misstep–perhaps your own–which is worth analyzing. I learned this the hard way when I strongly advocated for a typography change to a group of highly conservative clients. That experience taught me that focusing on broad, overarching themes during a pitch is far more effective than diving into specifics too soon, which can slow the process and raise red flags for potential clients.

NOT ALL PITCHES ARE THE SAME.
Some pitches require that we come armed with about ten pages or screenshots of how we would proceed with the project. Usually, a fee is charged for this, but one always wonders if any of the ideas stay in the background for "future referrals."

Other pitches are as cold as January in Helsinki: You arrive, you show the best of . . . you (hard to make those choices, but remember, five pieces are better than fifty), but oh, how painful it is to decide what to include and what to edit out of the presentation. You study the potential client, examine his needs, and see where your portfolio meets his expectations. When preparing for a pitch, be aware of cultural differences: Don't display your portfolio pieces with the bikini girls and the male models showing bare chests if you are in a country where such images are a no-no. Common sense and portfolio preparation must go together.

66 *The pitch may be the most pivotal moment in the life of the project, requiring the utmost preparation."*

DURING THE PITCH.

The day arrives, and you are ready to show these people that nobody does it like you and that they would be absolutely wrong and disappointed if they went with anyone but the one and only you. Of course, you don't say any of this directly. You infer it. Your portfolio pieces suggest this idea. And you tell them how you work, how you like people, and that you believe in collaborations. If you are not serious about these qualities, you should not be pitching.

I have never felt anxiety or lost sleep over a pitch. I will prepare. Period. You prepare as if it is the first time any of these people will see you or hear you—even if it's your tenth return trip. If you are already an experienced consultant, you don't rest on your laurels, which can be bloody thorny when trusted too seriously. There will always be people judging you in this gathering, people who have heard so much about you and think you are a legend, even a guru. Nonsense. A pitch is not the moment to go on autopilot. A pitch is where you pretend that this is your first presentation. This approach has always helped me work better at it.

Very important: The last sentence before you leave the room is key. Your last words stay with these people who can determine your destiny—at least, your momentary, immediate destiny.

Leave smiling. Remind them that no matter whom they select, the important thing is that they are taking the right actions by seeking help and going for a rethinking and that you, of course, would be honored to join them in their journey. Try to summarize the key takeaways you feel should be addressed to move the project forward, regardless of the consultant hired. A typical farewell statement sounds like this: "You have a challenge ahead of you to transform this newsroom into a more digital-driven organization. You have the right people, too, smart and enthusiastic. I know you will hire a consultant who not only teaches the team how to achieve their goals but also inspires them."

❝ *During the pitch make it clear that you are the best person for the job and explain why. The more specific reasons you offer, the better.*"

WAITING FOR THE VERDICT AFTER A PITCH.

After you leave the pitch session, don't go counting days until you hear from the potential client. Go about your business, put the pitch behind you, and be proud of what you did to secure the job, but don't go into overdrive about it. Easier said than done, especially when you really want the job.

Eventually, the phone rings. The first sentence from the spokesperson in charge of delivering the verdict says it all:

• If they say, "We have been so honored that you joined us for this pitch . . ." then it's the kiss of death. "Nice to have seen you, but we picked another consultant."

• If they say, "This was not an easy decision for us . . ." then it's the same sentiment put differently. They belabor the point that you and someone else were the finalists, but only one could be picked, and you already know it was not you. As honored as you may be to have placed a close second, you ain't it, kid.

Try telling the first runner-up in the Miss Universe contest that she was close to winning. She is returning to Ukraine, while Miss Venezuela gets a luxurious pad in New York City from where she shuttles around the world. I know, because I sat next to a Miss Venezuela-turned-Miss Universe during a long flight from Bangkok to Frankfurt. Perks of the traveling consultant.

And, of course, the nice clients call you. These are the ones whose mothers taught them good manners. On the other hand, there are those who never call you to give you the results of their verdict. To them, you are yesterday's linguini. In those cases, you hear who won the pitch through the rumor mill—or read about it in a blog (gasp). There is no excuse for this type of behavior. One usually loses to a worthy competitor who is probably going to do a great job, so I normally send a note to the prospect to say that they are indeed in good hands. In some cases, I am a friend of the winning consultant; I have even shared a glass of bubbly to celebrate the occasion with a competitor. Accentuate the positive.

After you hear the disappointing news that you are not the chosen consultant for the project, take twenty-four hours to study what went wrong. Was it the color of that tie I wore? Did I come across as inflexible? Then move on to your next project, plan the next pitch, and don't dwell on what could have been.

Sometimes you get that project later, on the rebound. Don't be too proud! Just get your trumpet out of its case, aim it to the skies, and get ready for your solo, the way Tio Kiko always did. This is America, the land of competition, and soon, another opportunity to pitch your services will appear. Let the mambo begin!

📋 MAKE A NOTE
Come to the Pitch Fully Prepared

You should prepare as if this is your first presentation, so don't rest on your laurels. This "first time" approach has always helped me to work better at it. A pitch is not the moment to go on autopilot. Very important: The last sentence before you leave the room is key. Everyone who listened to your pitch must feel that they would learn much from you.

GETTING THE JOB.

A prospective client has reached out to you via email, social media, and a phone call. There is a brief conversation that may go something like this: "Hi, Mario, I have a possible project that you may help us with. We think that we are lagging in our ability to do digital journalism well. We are still very print-oriented, and we know that, in the long run, our audience will be primarily consuming information on mobile devices. Can you help us?"

After a brief chat, which is part instructional—why more people are reading news on mobile devices—and part practical—my own current workload, future openings, dates for another call or visit—I then prepare a letter of intent. I find that it serves to establish objectives, set the scope of the project, define requirements of their team, and also provide an outline of potential deliverables and pricing. It helps set clear expectations on both sides and removes room for assumptions. A letter of intent to work together tends to be more of a personal icebreaker, which avoids the coldness and legalese of a formal contract at the start of the client/consultant relationship. Each firm has a different style for drafting contracts. Allow the client to send you their preferred contract format, then comply.

SHOULD THE CONSULTANT CHOOSE THE CLIENT?

Normally, clients choose the consultant. That is why we prepare our case and portfolios and go to pitch interviews. However, my friend and experienced consultant from Norway, Espen Egil Hansen, has a different take on this process. He questions why the clients get to choose who they wish to work with and not the other way around. Here is a transcript of Espen's take on the subject:

Don't let the customers pick you—you pick them!

Everyone understands that it is crucial for a customer to pick the right consultant, one who has the knowledge, resources, and stamina to effectively attack the problem the customer is facing. As a consultant, it is easy to be flattered by a request from a company with a great brand and market position. Also, it is easy to think that you will accept the job as long as you get your fee. However, I have learned (often the hard way) that I must be picky with what consulting gigs to accept. It's necessary to resist the initial temptation of saying yes and inflict on myself a mindset that I am the one to pick the customer—not the other way around.

To help me pick the right customers, I have developed a checklist of ten questions that I use actively before accepting a new offer. When I evaluate completed gigs, I surprisingly often find that there is a strong correlation between my ability to answer the questions with honesty and integrity and success in the project. Three of those questions appear here:

1. Am I substituting for a weak and insecure leader?

An absolute no-go for me is if I sense a CEO is seeking external validation for a decision that he or she knows is the right one but for some reason, doesn't dare to execute. It could be out of fear for how the employees, the board, or even customers will react to an unpopular decision. Typically, there are strong and conflicting views in a management group on what the right direction is. The CEO may lack the ability to turn this disagreement into positive friction where arguments are weighted against each other in the interest of the best possible solution. In some cases, the one that appears to be the leader is not the de facto–the leader making the final call. If the leader cannot decisively manage internal conflicts and relies on a consultant to endorse their decisions, the likelihood of creating lasting value is slim. Beware of becoming a scapegoat for weak leadership.

PS: Don't be blinded by charismatic, analytic, famous, or well-formulated leaders. These are all good virtues or tools to leverage in leadership. Still, they cannot substitute the most important task: The ability to make final decisions and get support from the surroundings to implement them.

2. Do the customers need a mentor rather than a consultant?
Being on the top is a lonely place. There is a tendency that only the problems that no one else in the organization can solve flow up to the CEO. There is little or no one to discuss the case with, and the result is that the poor CEO spends her time on frustrating and non-solvable problems. I have found that sometimes, what a CEO truly needs is not a strategy consultant but a mentor. CEOs often face unique, unsolvable problems and may benefit more from a long-term mentoring relationship than a specific consulting project. Mentoring and consulting are two very different roles (and cannot be combined working with one customer). With my background as a CEO and editor in chief, I found that I enjoy the mentor role and, with the right match, can help build long-term value from this position. While consulting typically is focused on a specific problem or outcome and is limited to a specific time, mentoring is more of a long-term personal relationship. The point is not to give advice but rather to be a listener, sparring partner, and sometimes the one asking tricky questions concerning the leadership role.

3. Is the problem already solved?

Sometimes, I am asked to investigate problems that I later learned have already been addressed by an internal project. It seems the idea is to have a second opinion by letting an independent outsider work on the problem and see if he ends up with the same conclusion. As a consultant, it is, of course, okay to review a strategy or conclusion of a project as long as this is an open, transparent premise from the very start. If, however, you get involved without knowing there have been earlier projects working on the same problems, there are slim chances of success. No one is really committed, and no one is willing to change positions. In short, it's not a real process, so stay away!

THE IMPORTANCE OF THAT FIRST MEETING.

The first meeting to kick off a project is key, a thought that I can't emphasize too much here. Indeed, while I have successfully offered my consulting services for over 750 projects in my career, I will never forget the one I did not get: a prominent newspaper title in the Northeast US.

This was early in my career—although by then I should have known better—and I was thrilled when this iconic newspaper contacted me for a complete redesign. I went to the library and got a book with the history of that newspaper. It was summer, and I reclined under an umbrella at the beach on the west coast of Florida, reading every word, savoring the rich history of a title that was part of American history. Then I flew to have my first meeting with the team.

My head was bursting with excitement and knowledge about this newspaper. I could identify the faces of the mustachioed characters in the lobby, and I could see early editions, complete with the six-column banner headlines. But I had nothing to show. I sat there and allowed myself to be interviewed, but I had nothing to show for how I would change this giant of journalism.

The moment I stepped out of the building, I knew that it had not been a good meeting. A few days later, I received the call that someone else had been selected to do the job. On the flight back, I was summarizing my own failure: Why did I not put together some mock-ups? Something to show the ideas that were already circling in my head!

I did not relax much at the beach the rest of that summer vacation. I simply could not get the sequence of events during that meeting out of my head. Revisiting such experiences is part of the learning process. This is when, no matter what you are doing—making your coffee, playing with your grandchildren, building sandcastles, applying sunscreen—all that you can do is deal with feelings of anger and self-doubt. How could I have not prepared better? Why did I spend my time reading the history of this newspaper and not let the design ideas in my head land on paper to show the team? Make mental notes. Learn from the experience.

Some three decades later, this is the one that got away. While I could tell myself that it was not meant to be—which is how my dear mother would justify when good things did not happen—I knew it was meant to be. I simply did not prepare properly. That experience forever changed my approach. I am proud to say that it has never happened again yet.

Lessons were learned, and I never again showed up for a first meeting without some tantalizing goodies to present to the clients. In fact, I have found myself preparing sketches only after having an occasional conversation with a potential client, even with no definitive date or a first meeting. Better to over-prepare anytime.

Always prepare well prior to this first meeting. Learn as much as possible about your client and this specific project. What are the goals? Read marketing reports. Study the client's website and social media output. Who are your client's competitors? In our type of consulting, with media companies, my team and I will turn to the competition's content and presentation, audience reach, and advertising revenue.

The first meeting is the first impression, even when you have already met with some of the principal players in the room that day. We do a detailed preparation for each client, even offering samples of how the client's products could be transformed. It is not about giving it all away but, in a way, offering tapas before they get to consume the full paella.

We also turn to the publication's archives: What is the trajectory of this brand as seen by the audience? I always tell myself, This publication survived x number of years without our collaboration, so what is it that makes the publication special? What are the elements of the product's legacy that can inspire us as we transform it and adapt it to the present?

The first meeting is the ideal moment to learn in detail what the client wishes to accomplish. What problem does the client say needs to be solved, and why? What does the client expect from us as consultants? How will the work be divided?

And importantly—who will be in the meeting? Knowing the cast of characters, their titles and influence, is quite helpful. Group dynamics are similar from project to project, but what is different is the makeup of the group—many alpha males in a meeting can be as disruptive as the absence of an alpha male and an overabundance of beta types with no opinions (hard to say which is worse).

Assess how realistic the goals—and the timelines—are, and then express your honest opinion about them. Plus, it is always helpful to hear from the clients why we have been selected to accompany them on this project journey.

The first briefing is also an opportunity for the consultant to get a sense of who is who among the top group of stakeholders. Inevitably, there will be one person present who does not agree that a consultant is needed for the project. By the time we arrive, this person's ideas have been overruled. The consultant is here, but that does not mean that this individual will be difficult to manage for the duration of the project.

Here is an example of someone from the in-house team who refused to let go of his beliefs, even when his superiors decided to move ahead with change. We had a project involving color in a traditionally black-and-white newspaper. The company that owned the newspaper had already approved the addition of color and invested in expensive color printing machines, but this senior editor did not believe in color and thought that the newspaper would lose its authoritative characteristic—what he referred to as "gravitas"—with the addition of colors.

At every step, and with every shade of even the faintest color, he raised his hand to say that it was too much. His colleagues would get into an argument with him right in the middle of our meetings. Remember the rules of the game: You are a guest in this house, so when the locals get into an argument with each other, you simply listen, interjecting yourself only when asked a direct question.

Eventually this newspaper launched its color edition, and the readers reacted positively (who does not like color? Life is in color!). Finally, this editor accepted that color was here to stay.

A few months later, I heard him at a media conference, on stage, saying, "When we introduced color to our newspaper. . ." He sounded happy. He was a proud presenter, and I couldn't help but smile. When all is completed, it is the client who has to live with the results, not the consultant. The good consultant has interpreted the dream so well that the client now lives it!

As consultants, we remember another basic occurrence—call it the evolution of an idea: First, a person in the team rejects your idea, then he accepts it because he is overruled, then, suddenly, it was his idea from the start! Celebrate that the idea is accepted.

The consultant must establish his credibility during this first meeting. Without displaying a resume on the screen, it does help to remind the group in a few short sentences why you were brought in. You must establish credibility quickly.

I find it helpful to relate one of my previous projects to the one I'm about to start with a new group. "This is how I tackled a similar problem," I will say, while showing images of that project reaching its successful completion. Meanwhile, I always remind my present clients that no two media houses are alike and that their project is unique, and we will tackle it as such.

The other side of this, which has happened to me several times, is when the clients present a challenge in their project that you have never encountered before. Never pretend to be an expert on everything.

Honesty and transparency are key here. "No, I have never made that type of conversion of a publication, but I am willing to dive into it, and together with your talented in-house team, we will discover how to solve the issue." There is something special about new challenges.

Remember that in the first meeting, clients are evaluating how you react, how you answer questions under pressure. The group will be looking at your body language. I prefer to stand up at the head of the conference room table. Be relaxed. Be cool. The consultant must navigate what could be turbulent waters. This is when the consultant acts self-assured, relying on expertise and experience, articulating the best answer for the questions asked, and trying not to deal with personalities.

Often, the top stakeholder—a CEO or owner of the media organization—expresses a strong opinion: "I would like very much for us to change the format of this product, start new, and create a more friendly, upbeat, and modern brand." While that may indicate a positive, open mind, and is usually music to our ears, this may be the first time that the other stakeholders in the room have heard about the CEO's position. A few faces may show shock. A courageous person may ask the CEO a question. By the end of this meeting, everyone should be in agreement as to what the clear goals of the project are, which leads to the "What's next?" question and the creation of a realistic timeline.

PREPARE A REPORT.
Soon after this meeting, and definitely within the next twenty-four hours, you will usually draft a report to send the client, outlining all that was discussed, then share highlights with your team.

Communication is key. The effective consultant keeps the lines of communication open, both with the client and the appointed project leader, as well as with those members of the consulting team who will be associated with the specific project.

Finally, arrive at the first meeting with a presentation that presents your views and philosophy but that weaves parts of the client's product and challenges into it. This secures better attention from the client and opens up a more fertile conversation. Avoid appearing like a rigid consultant who is simply saying, "This is how I do it, and you adapt to my style." The effective consultant appears flexible and open to new ideas and is a good listener to what the in-house project team has to say. You'll be surprised how many wonderful ideas come directly from what is already there. Remember, this company was there before you arrived.

Remember: The client understands his business better than anyone else. You are the outsider looking in. Also important is a point that Alan Weiss makes in his book: "All clients know what they want. Few know what they need. That difference is your value added." (2)

FIRST DAY OF A PROJECT.

Long before we become "friends" with our client and her team, we must get to the essentials. To me, the first day in the life of a project is key. While the people around the conference room table do not always know each other well, there is a common purpose: the successful completion of a project. Here is your chance to identify those with the best ideas.

On that first day, the consultant comes prepared to listen. I have often said that we earn a large portion of our consulting fee on the first day of the project. If the consultant listens carefully, makes mental notes, and envisions the many phases of the project, good results will follow.

Since my business is that of editorial design, I make sketches as the in-house team talks. Soon after that first meeting, I make sketches that provide 75 percent of what stays to the completion of the project. The consultant listens. The consultant internalizes the information. At that point in the project, the consultant has not been "contaminated" by the internal struggles and challenges of the house. You are still the outsider with experience and expertise, looking at the challenge in front of you but approaching it with an outsider's perspective–what the in-house people lack, and probably the reason you are there in the first place. What sketching does for me is what good note-taking does for the HR or IT consultant. Use whatever recordkeeping device works best. If I wish to jot down thoughts beyond the visuals, I turn to the Notes app in my iPhone and write key pieces of the conversation.

Tip: At the end of your day, revisit those notes and do a new set of "centerpieces from today's session." Usually, at that point, twelve items end up as three main centerpieces that will guide my process the next day, which I share with my team. The new consultant must develop her own way of recording what's essential, revisiting it, editing it, and ending up with what truly matters in the life of the project. On the first day, engage the client. Involve the client in the discovery process to ensure their perspective is considered. Listen well.

" *Curate your notes of that first-day meeting and identify the key centerpieces that you sense will be essentials to create a successful project.*"

PERSONAL NOTE
The Wall Street Journal

At **The Wall Street Journal,** I was commissioned to put color into one of the last newspaper holdouts of black-and-white fame. How do you begin transformation for a newspaper that dates back to 1889, in an environment that is not particularly welcoming of change? Grab a copy of **The Journal,** and the first thing you notice is the "What's News" column, with summaries of stories on page one. In my first briefing with them, I was informed that "What's News" is the most-read item on the front page, and it has been for almost a hundred years, so I made a mental note of that detail. That same day, we "colorized" that "What's News" column to a neutral beige from top to bottom, dominating the page totally.

The Journal designers in the room looked over my shoulder and told me, "That will never fly here. Remember, we are a black-and-white newspaper, and this is too much of a splash of color. And on the front page? Never." Change was to put color on the "What's News" column on the front page of **The Journal.**

I listened respectfully, went about finishing the colorization of that element on the computer, then printed the page and pinned it to the bulletin board in the art department. When the CEO serendipitously walked in to say hello, he glanced at that board and said: "That's just great. That color looks as if it belongs there."

Real, big change often occurs in the blink of an eye. Such was the case at **The Journal.** (3) I am happy that I arrived at that first briefing meeting ready to listen. Even today, when I find a copy of the print edition of **The Journal** stuck in the seat-back pocket of an airplane, I smile, thinking of that one small dramatic change that won the day •

ESTABLISH THE PROJECT GOALS EARLY.

Seasoned consultants, such as Roger Black, who have clients in media houses around the globe, believe in the importance of that first encounter with a project team: The essential part is the first phase, the brief. Here you establish the goals of the project: design, content, and business. Here are some of the items that the consultant should consider prior to that first meeting, which each consultant should adjust to serve his specific needs:

- Set the metrics of success, both for design and business.
- Study all the data: readers, users, and market.
- Define the culture (*l'esprit et la matière*).

- Define the design space.
- Determine the technical requirements.
- Assign employees to teams.
- Create a schedule.
- Review the budget.

When it comes time for the consultant to present ideas, it is best to follow some logistical steps to facilitate the discussion. The steps listed refer to my specific type of media consulting, but the themes and the idea of discovering as much as possible about the client and his product before a meeting are universal.

FIRST PRESENTATION OF IDEAS.
You have listened to a variety of voices and made notes of what you think is important, and now is the time for you, the expert, to present how you would deal with the challenges the project presents. For us, this is the design stage, when we show various options of how a newspaper website could look, always referring back to how the brief from the client inspired each specific visual option. Goal of this stage: Pick an option that indicates design direction.

SECOND PRESENTATION OF IDEAS.
Now that everyone has listened to the consultant's suggestions and the design options have been presented and discussed, the consultant returns with corrections and/or new suggestions. We call this the "prototype stage," where our designers have worked with the newspaper's designer to create what looks like a real newspaper or website. This will lead to a second round of revisions but gets closer to the final product. Goal: Prepare for the launch of the new project/ideas.

IMPLEMENTATION STAGE.
Now that the consultant's ideas have been presented, analyzed, edited, and turned into an almost-final product, it is time to set a timeline for implementation, with training of personnel as a key aspect of this stage. For us in design, we fill out all the details

and create a style book, a rule book that is now done in code but carefully documented in an outline. Technical tests are done, and everything is made ready for the launch, at least for the initial launch of the project. Focus groups may be conducted prior to launching the new product to make sure there will not be unpleasant surprises later. Goal: Launch—and celebrate!

These steps can be applied to any scale of project, including work I am doing for myself. If I forget to set the brief and go through the stages in order, the result always takes longer and sometimes starts going in circles. But working with the client's definitions of success and their culture, their data, and their team, the consultant can bring them along stage by stage because they have confidence that it is all working.

They understand that good media design takes a lot of work, including their own. That's ownership. At the end, the client must feel it was all their project, following their goals and ideas. And then it becomes their success.

GREAT IDEA
First Day Tip

Listen well and answer questions. Let your sound knowledge of your subject guide the conversations, while being aware that many of your clients may also be well educated on the subject. Recently, one of my clients told me, "We have had other consultants here who arrived with a thousand questions. Well, we want answers; that's why we hire consultants." It is okay to ask pertinent questions, but edit your list of questions and remember to pepper that first day's conversation with statements that reaffirm your expertise. At the end of the first day, your clients should share a happy hour, patting themselves on the back for selecting you to accompany them on this project. Cheers.

THE BEST IDEA WINS.
All this brings us back to a thought that has been the foundation of my consulting work for decades: A project is a team effort, and the best idea wins. Many people contribute to the success of a project, and ideas come from a variety of sources. As the chief architect of

my projects, I always begin with sketches of my vision for the project. Once I have done that, I usually tell members of my team, "Here are my initial doodles; add your ideas and see what happens." They usually do. I am always happily surprised. Surround yourself with people who are more talented than you, and everyone shines. As I look back at hundreds of my projects, I can always refer to a great visual detail that was contributed by a member of the project team. That best idea won. On the launch date, when the product is transformed, all the best ideas are there, a win-win situation.

DRAFTING CONTRACTS.
If there is one aspect of my work as a consultant that I dislike more than any other, it is the drafting of contracts. However, it is a necessary part of that moment where the consultant and client decide that they need each other. Then it is a matter of drafting a document that specifies how the collaboration will take place.

Each consultant has a different model for the drafting and execution of contracts. Clients usually do too, and the client's lawyers will often take part in drafting and reviewing the contract.

As I do many projects with foreign clients, I am always aware of tax regulations in the various countries and remind clients that the figure I quote them is not including taxes, as I pay taxes in the United States. In most cases, there is a form to fill out, and one must send the client abroad proof of paying taxes in the US. Better to take care of this before the client deducts taxes according to his country's tax laws—not a winning situation usually.

Consultants usually work in two contract modes: per-project contracts and retainer contracts. I work with both types of contracts. Sometimes one begins with a per-project contract. If a project has resulted in a successful collaboration with the team, then a retainer contract is signed, allowing for maintenance, continued coaching of the team, and the inevitable tweaks that take place once a project is launched.

TYPES OF CONTRACTS COMPARED

Contract type	Per-project contracts	Retainer contracts
Description	**A per-project contract** is an agreement where the consultant is hired to complete a specific task or project with a defined scope, deliverables, and timeline. Payment is typically rendered upon the completion of the project or at specified milestones.	**A retainer contract** is an ongoing agreement where the consultant is retained for a set period, usually with a recurring payment (monthly, quarterly, etc.). This type of contract often involves a commitment to a certain number of hours or tasks per month, providing continuous support and services.
Advantages	**Clear scope and deliverables:** The project has a defined beginning and end, with specific outcomes, making it easier to manage expectations. **Cost predictability:** Clients know the total cost up front, which can aid in budgeting. **Flexibility for consultants:** Once the project is completed, consultants are free to take on other work.	**Stable income:** Monthly or quarterly payments provide consistent cash flow for the consultant. **Long-term client relationship:** Ongoing engagement fosters deeper understanding and trust, potentially leading to more impactful work. **Flexible services:** Clients can have more fluid needs met without renegotiating terms for each task.
Disadvantages	**Inconsistent income:** Consultants face potential gaps between projects, leading to irregular income. **Limited client relationship:** Short-term engagements may not foster deep, long-lasting client relationships. **Scope creep risk:** Projects can often expand beyond the initial agreement, leading to additional unpaid work. **Higher pricing rate:** Smaller overall costs when compared to a retainer contract but likely a higher rate per task.	**Ambiguous scope:** Without clear boundaries, expectations can become unclear, leading to potential conflicts. **Client commitment:** Clients might be hesitant to commit to long-term contracts, especially if unsure of future needs. **Consultant availability:** Consultants need to ensure they can consistently provide the required level of service without overcommitting. **Larger budget impact:** These contracts typically carry higher overall price tags that smaller clients might shy away from, even though there is arguably greater overall long-term value.

PERSONAL NOTE
Ten Tips for Drafting Consulting Contracts

Overall, the best advice I can offer is to keep your contract as simple as possible but specific enough about deliverables, timelines, and who is responsible for the various steps of the project. Here are some tips for achieving this balance:

Clearly define the scope of work.
• It helps to begin with an overall statement that summarizes the main goal of the project and includes specifics:

> • For per-project contracts, outline specific tasks, deliverables, timelines, and milestones. For retainer contracts, describe the types of services provided monthly and any limitations or exclusions. Because today's technology allows for constant communication, it is wise to be specific: "Unlimited email consultations, one remote video call per week, etc." This should be phrased in a friendly way so as to not give the client the impression that you, the consultant, may be inflexible or difficult to communicate with. Confession: I seldom look back on a contract to count how many email or phone call exchanges I had with a client. Some clients are in need of continued hand-holding; others you must prompt to keep the communication going. It all balances out in the end.

Specify payment terms.
• Detail payment schedules, whether fixed fees for projects or monthly retainers. Many clients today prefer monthly retainers. Include clauses for late payments, additional charges for scope changes, and any up-front deposits.

> • If assigning payments to specific landmark moments of the project, specify as follows: first payment upon delivery of three design concepts. It is with great satisfaction that I can say, at least in the media consulting business, I've found clients are respectful of paying on time. It could have something to do with the fact that most media houses are landmark buildings in their cities and easy to locate in case there is failure to pay.

> • There was just one time when a client in South America failed to make the last payment at the conclusion of a project. I'd already given up on

collecting when ten years later, at a media conference in San Juan, Puerto Rico, my wife and I were dancing after an awards dinner. Suddenly, another couple on the dance floor kept moving toward us. It was the owner of that South American media company. He took an envelope from his inside jacket pocket, gave it to me, and said: "Sorry about the delay!" It was a sweet dance that night.

Set performance metrics and KPIs.
• Define how success will be measured. For projects, set clear deliverable acceptance criteria. For retainers, establish regular reporting intervals and metrics to evaluate performance. Today's technology allows for data to back up any narrative about a project's success.

Include a detailed timeline.
• For projects, provide a schedule with key milestones and deadlines. For retainers, outline expected response times and the frequency of service delivery. Be prepared for timelines to run into delays, and be flexible to accommodate some. My philosophy has always been to make sure that our **García Media** team fulfills its timeline promises, knowing too well that such may not be the case with the client. When the clients delay with their performance, I respectfully and gingerly send reminders every two weeks or so, sometimes having to break with hierarchical concerns and going all the way to the CEO to make sure that "we still have a project."

Establish communication protocols.
• Specify preferred communication methods, regular schedule updates, and points of contact for both parties. For consultants today, in an environment of 24/7 communication, parameters must be set in terms of hours of available email/phone consultations, for example. If working with international clients, be specific about your hours of availability in consideration of local time zones.

Outline termination clauses.
• Describe conditions under which either party can terminate the contract, notice periods required, and any penalties or refunds applicable.

Define intellectual property rights.

• Clarify who owns the intellectual property created during the contract. For projects, ensure deliverable ownership is clear. For retainers, specify ownership of ongoing work and materials.

Address confidentiality and nondisclosure.

• Include confidentiality clauses to protect sensitive information shared during the consulting engagement. Reassure your clients that all communication is confidential. After years of consulting, I usually tell my clients on the first day: "Whatever we discuss stays in this room. I have not lasted five decades as a consultant by discussing my clients' secrets. For me to do my job effectively, I must get inside your kitchen, so to speak, and see how you cook. All that stays with me, period." That also applies to the human dramas that are likely to occur before the consultant's eyes. I often think that a good **Netflix** series could be based on the memories of a consultant intricately involved inside the top media houses of the world. Good material, for sure. Guaranteed entertainment with drama and suspense.

Review and update regularly.

• Periodically review and update contracts to reflect changes in scope, services, or legal requirements. Ensure both parties agree to and sign any amendments. Good client relations rely on transparency and clarity.

Tip: Allow for the occasional extra hand-holding with a member of the project team, the one who calls you on a Sunday afternoon petrified with what will happen during the Monday morning meeting. Asking to be paid for an extra two hours of counseling a distraught client is not a good idea •

WHAT TYPE OF CONTRACT WORKS BEST?

The choice between per-project contracts and retainers depends on various factors:

• **Project complexity and duration:** For well-defined, short-term projects with clear deliverables, per-project contracts work well. For ongoing, evolving needs, retainers offer flexibility and continuity.

· **Client and consultant preferences:** Some clients prefer the predictability of project-based work, while others value the continuous support of retainers. Similarly, consultants may prefer the stability of retainers or the flexibility of project work.

· **Nature of services:** Consulting services that require ongoing support, strategy development, or continuous improvement are better suited for retainers. Projects with distinct goals and end points fit well with per-project contracts.

Ultimately, the best approach depends on the specific needs and circumstances of the client and consultant. Flexibility and clear communication are key to ensuring both types of contracts serve their intended purposes effectively. And just like no two projects are identical, neither are the contracts that define how the work will be executed.

MAKE A NOTE
First the Contract, Then the Team Effort

Contracts are a necessary part of the consulting process. Our clients require them to establish rules, define deliverables, and have a formal protocol that dictates how the various steps of the consulting process are followed. While drafting contracts has never been a favorite part of my duties, they are an inevitable part of the consultant's work, and I have even created a template, knowing well that each project is different. For instance, it's common for clients to engage their lawyers to draft contracts that adhere to organizational protocols and, when working internationally, the various regulations of tax laws for different countries. Once the contract is signed, the real work begins. While the contract may be between you, the consultant, and the firm authorizing the work, a widely assorted cast of players contributes to the success of a project, and ideas come from a variety of sources. The best idea wins, and when that happens, everyone benefits.

Tools of the Consultant

I **start each day with a cup of Nespresso Colombia coffee, usually in front of a Zoom screen with seven members of a project team staring at me from various locations. In the era of remote work, there is the occasional glimpse of a cat walking across the lap of a team member or a toddler who curiously looks at the screen. Indeed, this is different from when I started my consulting career.**

There was a time when a notebook, a good pen, and occasional phone calls were the tools available to keep track of projects and to communicate with the project team. Then along came those faxes that would allow for an instant graphic or notification to be exchanged between client and consultant. I woke up in many hotels around the globe immediately looking under the door to see if Client A had sent what she promised.

Then I would draw a sketch, even before my first cup of coffee, to respond and offer feedback. While technology has provided us with better tools to do our jobs, the two essentials of effective consulting remain the same:

- Make a plan and a timeline.

· Keep communication lines open at all times.

To this day, I keep my notebook and pen handy. That's as basic as tools will ever get, but they are still necessary. I also make sure to start my day with a clear view of where my projects are and what must be tended to that day. Part of my methodology involves an imaginary stove.

That is how I see my agenda. Four burners: one hot, one medium, one low, one simmer. Each day I prioritize the day's tasks according to my imaginary stove. The hot item must be my priority, the others I tend to as time allows. The formula works for me.

Tools and Techniques for Effective Consulting

Project Management and Communication

In the fast-paced world of consulting, effective project management and seamless communication are the backbones of success. Over my fifty-five-year consulting career, I've witnessed the evolution of these tools and have embraced a few that I consider indispensable:

• **Project management software:** Tools like Asana, Trello, and **monday.com** have revolutionized the way consultants manage projects. These platforms offer comprehensive features such as task assignments, deadlines, progress tracking, and collaboration spaces. Asana, for instance, allows consultants to create detailed project timelines with Gantt charts, ensuring every team member stays on track and informed.

• **Communication platforms:** Efficient communication is paramount in consulting, where clarity and speed can make or break a project. Tools like Slack, Microsoft Teams, and Zoom have become industry standards. Slack's channel-based messaging system promotes organized and topic-specific discussions, reducing the clutter of traditional email chains. Meanwhile, Zoom has set the benchmark for virtual meetings, providing high-quality video conferencing that keeps global teams connected.

• **Document collaboration:** Google Workspace and Microsoft 365 offer powerful tools for document collaboration. Google Docs and Sheets enable real-time coediting and commenting, making it easier for consultants and clients to work on documents simultaneously, regardless of their locations.

Data Analysis and Visualization

Data is the new oil, and in consulting, the ability to analyze and visualize data effectively can set a consultant apart from the competition. Here are some tools and techniques that have proven invaluable:

• **Data analysis software:** Tools like Tableau, Power BI, and Python's Pandas library offer powerful data analysis capabilities. Tableau and Power BI provide intuitive interfaces for creating interactive dashboards that help clients understand complex data through visual storytelling.

• **Statistical analysis:** For more in-depth statistical analysis, consultants often turn to tools like R and SPSS. These platforms allow for advanced statistical modeling and hypothesis testing, which can be crucial in making data-driven decisions.

• **Visualization techniques:** Effective data visualization is not just about creating beautiful charts but also about telling a story. Techniques like heat maps, scatter plots, and network diagrams can provide insights that raw data alone cannot. Edward Tufte's principles of data visualization stress the importance of clarity, precision, and efficiency in presenting data. [1]

● Functional use of graphics is also key, as Nigel Holmes, who served for many years as **TIME** Magazine's graphics director, repeatedly instructed artists in attendance at his workshops internationally: "If you don't assign a meaning to everything in your graphic, the reader will." [2]

Innovative Methods for Problem-Solving and Ideation

Innovation is at the heart of consulting, requiring creative problem-solving techniques that can break through traditional barriers.

> • **Design thinking:** A human-centered approach to innovation, design thinking involves five stages: empathize, define, ideate, prototype, and test. This iterative process encourages creativity and ensures solutions are tailored to user needs. Companies like IDEO (ideo.com) have championed this method, showing its effectiveness in diverse fields.

MY OWN METHODOLOGY.

My own methodology for media projects is usually made up of four stages:

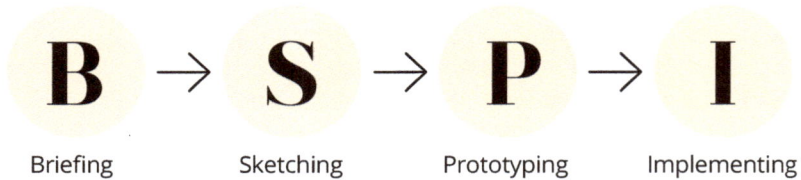

$$\textbf{B} \rightarrow \textbf{S} \rightarrow \textbf{P} \rightarrow \textbf{I}$$

Briefing   Sketching   Prototyping   Implementing

Let me explain a bit about each of these phases of a project within the context of media redesign transformations, though they are adaptable and applicable to a variety of other fields and projects.

Briefing. This is the mapping stage of the project, which allows for all involved to navigate subsequent steps more easily. Here, I use a variety of strategies. It is the first day of my meeting with the in-house team. Before we talk about how this product may look at the end of the project, we need to evaluate it in its present form. One of the exercises I sometimes use is to ask the group: If this publication were an animal, what type of animal would it be? I am always surprised to hear from two colleagues, veterans of the organization, who offer distinct views—one would say a horse, the other one a kitten. Those exercises help the consultant gauge what those creating the product think. Then I get into the question: In a perfect world, after a transformation, what type of animal should this publication be? That generally leads to a very proactive discussion.

Sketching. Once I have had a thorough briefing, I am ready to sit down with my team to sketch concepts of how this product could be transformed. This is the most creative phase of the project, and I have often thought that this is what I am paid to do. The consultant brings an outside perspective that, together with the knowledge and specific insights of those in the organization, can provide a recipe for what I think of as saluting the past with a firm hand but reaching out to the future with the potential of what could be.

I return to show our ideas to the clients, normally two or three versions deep, from which we emerge with a new version that often combines elements from all the iterations shared.

Prototyping. Armed with new sketches that have been analyzed and agreed upon by all, we get into the third phase, which is creating models of how the product could be. Here is how your website or your app may work. There is the element of surprise, but one can also immediately get a sense of how the in-house team reacts. Those prototypes will be tested with potential users for further deliberations and new iterations. Once a final model has been created, then the rest is the logistics of getting the product to market and the final step: implementation.

Implementing. Many pieces need to come together for a publication to launch with a new look or product. Developers must code the new styles into the content management system. Designers must prepare style sheets for all to become familiar with new typographic and color palettes. The product that is launched is going to be somewhat different ninety days later, after everyone has had a chance to test it with real content for real audiences in real time.

66 *The implementation of a project is the culminating point, the finish line of that 26.2-mile marathon, and, when the project has been successfully executed, the time to step up to the stage and get the good feedback and accolades."*

SOME OTHER POPULAR METHODS

Resource	Details
Mind Mapping	**Tony Buzan's mind mapping technique** is a powerful tool for brainstorming and organizing thoughts. By visually mapping out ideas, consultants can explore connections and uncover new insights that linear thinking might miss. (3)
SWOT Analysis	**A classic yet effective tool, SWOT analysis helps** consultants and clients identify strengths, weaknesses, opportunities, and threats related to a project or business strategy. This framework provides a structured approach to evaluating internal and external factors that can impact success. (4)
Six Thinking Hats	**Edward de Bono's Six Thinking Hats method** encourages parallel thinking by assigning different perspectives to different "hats." This technique fosters comprehensive analysis by separating thinking into manageable segments—facts, emotions, critical judgment, positive thinking, creativity, and process control. (5)

By leveraging these tools and techniques, consultants can enhance their efficiency, foster innovation, and ultimately deliver greater value to their clients. As technology continues to evolve, staying updated with the latest tools and methodologies will remain a crucial aspect of effective consulting. In addition, always using your notebook and pen as essential tools will seldom fail you.

OWNERSHIP.

Who owns the project? The consultant must make every effort to let the client and their team own the project. For that to happen, the team must get its hands in there. With the launch of project after project, I have witnessed how when the team's ideas are filtered into the final product, there is a greater sense of ownership, and thus, the project succeeds more readily. In the end, the best ideas win, regardless of their origin.

Some of my fellow consultants agree. Veteran media design consultant Roger Black is aware of the importance of ownership on the part of the client and wrote this in an email to me:

. . . working with the client's definitions of success, their culture, their data, and their team, the consultant can bring them along stage by stage because they have confidence that it is all working.

They understand that good media design takes a lot of work, and a lot of that is their own. That's ownership. At the end the client must feel it was all their project, following their goals and ideas. And then it becomes their success. (6)

TOOLS OF THE WORK
The Three Essentials of Effective Consulting

Today, consultants have technological tools to support every step of a project. However, at the start of my career, such tools were not available. While technology has improved our ability to do the job, the two essentials of effective consulting remain unchanged: (1) Create a clear plan with a realistic timeline. (2) Ensure the project team adheres to it, which is often a challenge, and maintain open lines of communication at all times. With today's remote communication tools, such as video calls, it is essential for consultants to use these platforms to address project questions one at a time, saving time and streamlining processes. Effective consultants also leverage a powerful psychological tool: ensuring clients feel ownership of the project. When a consultant departs at the end of a project, the best guarantee of long-term success is that the team working with the new concept feels they were part of its creation. While technology can save time, a consultant's most valuable tool remains their ability to advance the project through meaningful human interaction.

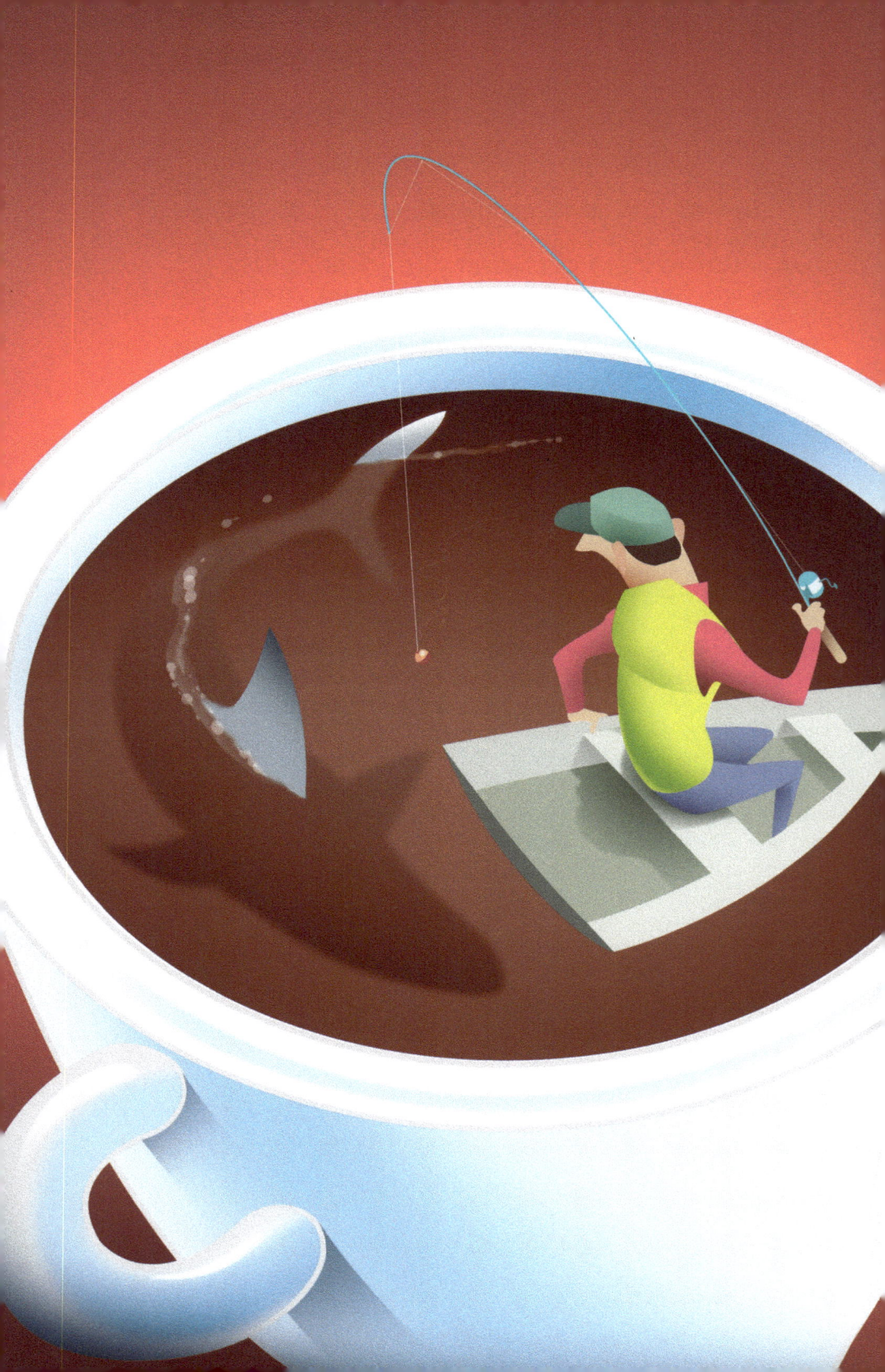

Rejection Is Always on the Menu

Rejection is part of what the consultant must accept. **Not that it becomes easier to do so with years of experience. It is best to analyze rejection and learn lessons from it. I have always given myself about twenty-four hours to do the mourning when an idea is not well received, or, worse, when a pitch results in a "thank you for your time, but we have decided to go with a different consultant."**

Of course, we all have different coping mechanisms to deal with rejection. In his book *Flawless Consulting: A Guide to Getting Your Expertise Used,* Peter Block offers practical advice on how to face rejection. He reminds us that resistance is a natural part of the consulting process and suggests the following:

• Understand the roots of resistance: Recognize that resistance often stems from fear or discomfort. Block emphasizes that resistance often stems from emotional reactions, such as fear, anxiety, or insecurity.

Clients might resist because they feel threatened by change, fear losing control, or worry about the implications of the consultant's recommendations. Understanding these emotional underpinnings is crucial for addressing resistance effectively.

> • Address concerns directly: Engage in open conversations about resistance to understand and mitigate it.

> • Build alliances: Identify and work with allies within the client organization to facilitate change. (1)

Building alliances is key, especially when you believe that the idea just rejected has merit and could be key to taking the project forward. That's when you identify and work with allies within the project group that you know are tuned in to your proposal.

If that fails, however, it is time to let go and present new ideas. I have seen an idea that was first rejected get full acceptance after members of the in-house team pushed for it. I could also fill a drawer with ideas that I thought had merit but were quickly rejected. That is one reason I remind my graduate students at Columbia University not to get too attached to their ideas. It is a life of pain and suffering ahead for anyone who does that. Better to realize that there are many other, often better, ideas where that original one came from.

WHEN YOUR IDEA WON'T FLY.
Consultants should approach rejection with empathy and validation. By acknowledging the client's feelings and concerns, consultants can create a supportive environment where clients feel heard and understood. This helps reduce defensiveness and opens up the possibility for constructive dialogue.

Block suggests that resistance might indicate a need for the consultant to adjust her methods or strategies. (2) This could involve changing the pace of the intervention, providing additional information, or revisiting the scope of the project to ensure it aligns with the client's comfort level and readiness for change. I have always taken pride in the fact that of the initial ideas my team and I present on that first day of a project, about 75 percent stay through to the end of the project. This is the result of having paid attention to the client briefing and situation. But that still leaves 25 percent of the ideas presented that are quickly abandoned. Often, some of the consultant's favorite ideas are in this 25 percent. The consultant looks at the rejected ideas, evaluates the importance they may have in the overall life of the project, and either transforms them, leading to acceptance, or abandons them in search of new, more desirable solutions.

IT HELPS TO KEEP A DIARY: DON'T LET THE MOMENT ESCAPE.
The occupation of consulting is one that lends itself ideally to keeping a diary of our adventures. The fact that we don't sit in the same office with the same skyline view all the time or that we enjoy happy hours and meals with many individuals of diverse backgrounds provides enough material to jot down a sentence here and there about what we observe. Undeniably, we have a front-row seat in the theater of the human condition. If your consulting project involves creative types—as many will—then you have yourself a ticket to a show worthy of Broadway.

While I did not set out to write a literary diary, I now am the proud owner of about 200 notebooks, some dusty and stuck to each other after years of cohabitating in humid confines, moving with me from place to place. I was often tempted to discard these during one of the moves, but once I sat on the floor of an empty room and started reading, I changed my mind. Good thing, as I revisited the diaries often when writing this book. My diaries included the agenda of each day but also observations and lessons learned that I would document before retiring at night.

It was fun to review some of them now, decades later, and I am grateful to my scribbles for reminding me of what a fantastic and wild ride this consulting journey has been but also for accentuating the lessons that I share here. These diaries are a cocktail that mixes bliss, frustration, rejection, and pure serendipity—all are on the menu for the consultant. The best part was seeing the sketches I would draw during a briefing meeting and realizing how many of those ideas first sketched in a conference room made it all the way to the end of the project. If there is such a thing as the biography of an idea, the diary entries are a sort of birth certificate worth keeping. Here is a sampling of some of those:

**WHEN THE CLIENT IS TRANSPARENT
(DES MOINES, IOWA, USA, 1991).**

The Des Moines Register

In 1991, I was in Des Moines, Iowa, on my first day of a new project. The one person in the room with more ideas—and definitely most ready to go—was the editor of the paper, Geneva Overholser. Then I met the editorial page editor, Dennis Ryerson, and found that he was so enthusiastic and eager to change the visuals of the opinion section that he thought it would be a good idea to start with the opinion page for this project.

Nothing beats enthusiasm in the early stages. Why not? I had never started with an editorial page, but this was the chance to do so. I had to seize the enthusiasm of this one editor, then the others would follow. In my notes, I wrote: "You have to love this editor, Geneva Overholser. Yesterday, she came to me and said, 'Mario, I think I am supposed to like what you are showing us, but I don't. Now, tell me why I should.'" Of course, I did—convinced her.

I wish more clients would be that transparent. Remember, as a consultant in dialogue with the main stakeholders of a company, you are interacting with educated people, many of whom take pride in reminding you of their pedigrees, and some who you will quickly realize are smart and real experts at what they do.

Convincing them is a challenge, but it can be done if you prepare your case. When the client asks you why you propose a certain strategy—or, in our case, a specific typographic font—don't use vague statements such as "because I like it." These people expect more from the consultant they hired. They expect good reasoning, statements that are backed up by studies, and, of course, if appropriate, why the strategy worked for you with a previous client.

❝ *Don't be afraid to alter the order of the steps in a project to take advantage of specific circumstances. While you should have a template for how to organize a project, it should be ready to be altered as needed.*"

WHEN THE CLIENT DELIVERS THE SKETCH OF THE PRODUCT AT THE FIRST MEETING (DUSSELDORF, GERMANY, 1999).

I'm in Germany, and I am back at the hotel. After the first day with the editors at **Handelsblatt**, I sense this will be a tough job. The chain-smoking editor with the scarlet nail polish pulled a paper dummy sketch of how she envisioned a redesign of her newspaper, Germany's financial daily.

My job is to change the format from a giant broadsheet of five wide columns to a more modern and playful seven-column grid. I must be diplomatic, take a look at the editor-made mock-up—a chamber of horrors—and interpret what she meant with her scribbles. The smell of cigarettes in that office is as offensive as her attempts at designing sketches.

WHEN THE CLIENT IS IN SHOCK
(TUCUMAN, ARGENTINA, 1994).

I'm in northern Argentina and today at the publisher's home, amid the spectacular scenery of Tafí del Valle, two hours by car from Tucuman, where the newspaper is headquartered.

The publisher decided that I should show my first design concepts away from the office while looking at the mountains. Not too shabby. We had alfresco lunch today, with delicious Argentinian *empañadas* (meat-filled pastries). The editors were shocked with my concepts.

Here was a group of key editors who had never seen a drop of color in their newspaper, suddenly faced with several boards of colorful pages.

And a new typeface (gasp). I am happy to see that at the end, editors were raising glasses of a good Mendoza Murloc and saying "*Arriba!*"

WHEN THE INITIAL LOOK AT THE PRODUCT MAKES YOU WANT TO RUN (SÃO PAULO, BRAZIL, 1993).

O ESTADO DE S. PAULO Oh my God, this is São Paulo. I am in the car from the airport to the city. Are all fourteen million citizens of this giant city out in the street today? Giant city. Giant newspaper, **O Estãdo de S. Paulo.** I categorize the product as a two -headed monster: headline runs into headline here, many texts on front page, photos compete in sizes.

I think I will wait till I take a shower and nap a bit before I start some sketching to show the editors at the first meeting tomorrow. When a project presents what appear to be major challenges and obstacles, it is best to tackle those as early as possible. Every project has its fun aspects, and we gravitate to handle those first. However, I have found out that it is best to get the majorproblems on the table first, as it usually leads to discussions and solutions faster.

WHEN YOUR IDEAS ARE NOT ACCEPTED (LISBON, PORTUGAL, 1992).

Diário de Notícias It is 1992–a bad day in Lisbon. I need to reach for a second glass of bubbly. I was here on my first day on this job to give a presentation of how the iconic **Diario de Noticias** could be reinvented. I was in the middle of what I thought was an inspiring slideshow about "the modern newspaper" when one of the older editors approached the front of the room.

With a tightened fist, and demonstrably angry, he pounded on the screen as I showed a page from an American newspaper that showed "how to do it right with color." "I don't believe in any of this," said the angry editor. "This is all cosmetic rejuvenation, and I don't think our newspaper needs this." The show was stopped. I sipped my sparkling water and contemplated the bubbles rising from the bottom of the glass, asking myself: Where do we go from here? I thought of heading for the door and getting on a plane home. I looked out the window and saw an imposing statue of one of Portugal's patriots rising proudly in the middle of a rotunda that was engulfed by the midday flow of traffic. Cars beeped their horns, and jets approaching the nearby airport flew overhead. I had a few seconds to continue the show, compose myself.

The sequel: The show went on, indeed. It took weeks to clear the air. The newsroom was divided, and those opposing the redesign left, including the editor. A new, youthful editor arrived, who quickly formed his own team. It was an early example of what I maintain today.

Sometimes, these consulting projects result in cadavers on the floor. Like the ancient Portuguese navigators, the new team set out to conquer, and in a record four months and a day, the new **Diario de Noticias** debuted with color, new typography, and a well-planned series of supplements. I learned in this project that sometimes the evolutionary rocess does not work. Instead, a revolution is what the doctor prescribes.

REJECTION IN BERLIN (GERMANY, 1994).

Berlin, 1994–Tough job here. Editor is extremely conservative. Does not want photos on the upper half of the front page, except on Mondays to promote a sports story. What's the reasoning here?

How can I move the editor beyond this limiting strategy for visuals on the front page? Seems difficult. The editor does not want change and yesterday asked me to take a day off and simply tour historic Berlin. What to do? I must create an art department here, to start a sense of visual culture. I am visiting the Bauhaus Museum for inspiration. Those Bauhaus guys had to break rules. My visit yesterday was like taking a bath in the essence of a movement that defines minimalism–the skeletal as elegant–and a mix of bright and pastel colors systematic in its approach to contrast.

THE CONSULTANT'S CRY OF DESPAIR
(SANTA FE, ARGENTINA, 2005).

Nov. 15, 2005–"God help me endure this." That entry into my diary at 10:26 a.m. summarizes the feeling of frustration when the client–also the company's owner–decides to go into a long lecture about typography, a subject he knows nothing about.

For forty-five minutes this man told the project team about fonts that work and why, discussing sizes and weights, but all with a helicopter perspective. At one point, he pulled from his pocket a bottle of cough syrup and said, "I like these letters on the bottle." Then, turning to me: "Mario, is there something similar we could use for headlines here?"

> *Sometimes, the top boss of the firm that has engaged you to offer expertise makes sure everyone knows that he is the real expert."*

> *What to do? Simply, listen and pick your battles. Allow the boss to have his time at the podium and then you show why you are the expert."*

What is the consultant to do when confronted with a situation like this? First, be diplomatic. You are the guest in the house, and he owns the place. Second, as quickly as possible, correct the misinformation about typography that has been distilled in the past hour.

Then take a look at the cough medicine container and gently say that, while you think that particular brand of cough medicine is good to cure your cough, the type itself is too bold and festive for headlines.

Fortunately, there are always enough smart minds in the room to appraise the presentations and come to conclusions.

And, of course, the CEO is rarely convinced. In cases like this, when all else fails, common sense prevails. Avoid letting such an incident become a crisis.

YOU GET HIRED, YOU CREATE, PROJECT DOES NOT COME TO FRUITION (DIE WELT, GERMANY, 2006).

I am sketching and sketching again for this title, but I get the sense that there is no urgency, as if the project is half-hearted, but here I am, talking to the attentive editor. My instinct tells me this is not going anywhere. (Epilogue: Project was not completed. My sketches remain in my diary forever. Some projects end up in a drawer. You move on.) It disheartening to see your ideas consigned to the dustbin of the unused, yet this, too, is an inevitable part of a consultant's journey.

Norman Lear's Precious Mantra: "Over and Next". The late Norman Lear, the gifted creator of such iconic TV sitcoms as *All in the Family, The Jeffersons, Maude,* and *Mary Hartman.* Mary Hartman lived by a mantra that was narrowed down to two words: over and next. He described the space/time in between over and next as a hammock, or as "this moment." As a consultant, I think that Lear's mantra can be a valuable reminder, especially on days when things are not going as planned or desired. I remember wishing I had a hammock to lie in at several points during my career. Over and next: Let's not forget those two words.

WHEN MENTALITY CHANGES DRAMATICALLY (LAKE KONSTANZ, GERMANY, 1993).

1993—My runs here around Lake Konstanz are peaceful and inspiring. Ironically, on my first day here today with this team we sat to discuss the modernization of Südkurier in a building with a mural painted by monks centuries before. There was a long wooden table, probably used as a dining room table in the past. I don't know if it was this old ambience, but I sensed that the mood of the editors in the room was not very enthusiastic about change. The editor in chief asked me if I was sure a color photograph on the front page of a newspaper that had never used color would have any impact. (Epilogue: By the time of my second visit, the team had already moved to their new headquarters, with no hidden corners for monks wanting a moment of meditation, no murals on the walls with tales of winemakers of another era. Instead, a glass cage—a large entrance hall with lots of steel and modern, black furniture—and upon entering, the visitor would see a lineup of futuristic television screens hanging from silver tubes, each showing a different channel. Indeed, **Südkurier** had switched channels and buildings—and mentality.)

WHEN LESS IS BEST
(ATHENS, GREECE, 1993).

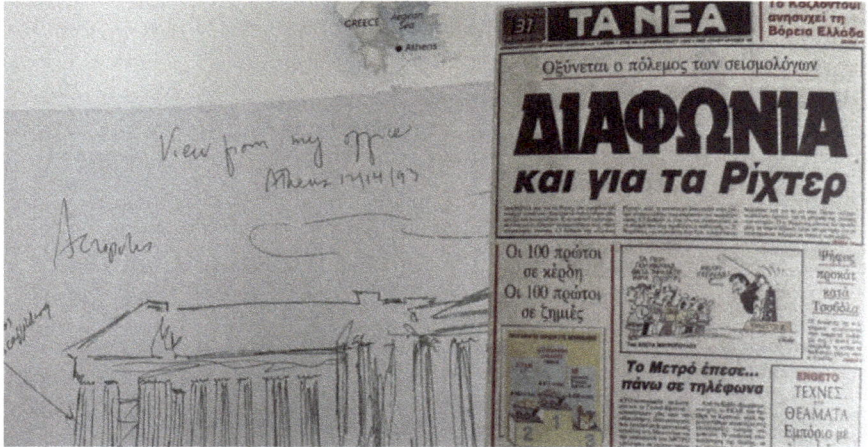

1993–Passing by Greece's Parthenon, which is undergoing repairs, "a facelift," our project leader told me. Well, what a coincidence that **Ta Nea,** the iconic Greek newspaper, has invited me for a facelift and repairs too. The challenge is that the Greek alphabet presents new territory to be explored for me. I have recently been putting color in newspapers. Here, I have to diplomatically suggest that they tone down the colors if they wish to wear the crown of Greece's leading, authoritative newspaper. The consultant's challenge: diplomatically conveying that a client's current practice contradicts the company's core values, while tactfully phrasing the critique to avoid making the client feel foolish Precision in language is paramount.

❝❝ *My diary entries remind me of how uniquely different each project is, not only because of the geographic location and culture, but, especially, the people assigned to work with the outside consultant. Navigating the challenges of the human condition is key for the successful completion of projects."*

CREATING SOMETHING NEW (SINGAPORE, 1988).

1988–I am jet-lagged after the long flight from home to Singapore. I am hungry for a full meal during the breakfast buffet here. The Cuban in me reaches for the rice bowl, puts fried eggs on top, a piece of meat, and it is like what my mom would make for lunch or dinner. It is not just your mind that must adapt to a new environment.

At dinner time, I want to have granola and milk. But I am excited to come here not to rethink a product but to create a new one, **The New Paper.** What an opportunity to bring all those ideas that you think make for a modern newspaper and that are often rejected in legacy projects.

I have a great, experienced editor who thinks modern, Peter Lim, and an experienced, very visual art director, Peter Ong. We have some rules and formats to follow, so I told these agents that we would apply systematic creativity here. Rethinking an existing product can be tough, but there's nothing quite like the thrill of building something totally new from the ground up.

💡 GREAT IDEA
Acceptance and Rejection

As you have seen through my diary entries, there are days when the most tried-and-true methodology that has worked for the consultant before is just not going to cut it elsewhere, thus the concept of approaching each project as unique. No two are alike. At the end of a typical month, the consultant has gone from bliss to rejection. It is all part of the job. We learn from both experiences.

The Mindset of the Consultant

J ust like each project is different, each consultant is an individual, with a unique personality, who brings a set of values, behaviors, and life experiences. This is what is referred to as the consultant's "mindset."

WHAT IS THE MINDSET OF A CONSULTANT?

In general terms, these are five mindset characteristics that effective consultants display. I admit that the concept of consultants having a mindset is fascinating, so I have turned to fellow veteran consultants– sometimes my competitors as we pitched for the same jobs–to try to understand if there is some general mindset. Before we get to those consultants' reflections on the concept of mindset, here are five traits that are generally associated with the mindset that sets effective consultants apart, enabling them to navigate complexity, foster collaboration, and deliver impactful results across diverse projects and client environments:

· **Adaptability and flexibility:** Effective consultants are adept at adapting to different client needs, project requirements, and changing circumstances. They can pivot strategies and approaches as necessary to achieve desired outcomes. They don't arrive at a first meeting with a plan and rules set in stone.

• **Empathy and emotional intelligence:** Understanding and empathizing with clients' perspectives allows consultants to build trust, navigate complex interpersonal dynamics, and tailor solutions that resonate with stakeholders.

• **Analytical and critical thinking:** Consultants rely on analytical skills to assess data, identify patterns, and make informed decisions. Critical thinking enables them to evaluate problems from multiple angles and devise innovative solutions.

• **Resilience and persistence:** Projects may face setbacks or challenges, but resilient consultants remain focused on goals, maintain optimism, and persist in pursuing solutions despite obstacles.

• **Continuous learning and curiosity:** Embracing a growth mindset, effective consultants are curious about industry trends, new technologies, and evolving best practices. They prioritize continuous learning to stay relevant and offer cutting-edge insights to clients.

Effective consultants develop templates for what works and what doesn't, but those templates are set on wheels—for motion and for flexibility. Don't create formulas that you take from job to job. A methodology that worked in one project may backfire in another.

There have been numerous times that, upon leaving the site of a project and while flying at 35,000 feet and staring at the always-fascinating cloud formations, I would tell myself: Wouldn't it be fantastic if I could take the art director in my Project A, the technical support of Project C, and the management team from Project D? That's just cloud meditating. When I landed, I'd be aware that I had to work with the reality of the next project, but I would try to dig deeper into the cloud meditation thinking: What made the art director of Project A such an effective partner for that project? What separated the management team from Project D? That was a helpful process to get me to create a specific methodology—a template—for future projects. Apply the lessons learned, but never create a formulaic approach.

Each project begins with a blank page or two. To me, this is a healthier approach, and a fairer one for the client who hired me. Believe me, clients can smell a consultant's cookie-cutter approach from a mile away. Another reason why coming prepared to a first meeting with some specific examples–in our case, simple mock-ups of how the client's product could look–helps in the process of showing that you are thinking individually about this client, customizing his needs from the very onset of the project. "This is impressive that you captured so much of what we want to do already, at this stage of the project," a project manager told me recently. That is when this client's unique template is developed. After that, you can then apply your tried-and-tested methodology for other aspects of the project. If we consultants are interpreters of dreams, then it helps to show portions of the dream as early as possible. Remember, every dream is different.

Sometimes, as we interpret the client's dreams, it is also our job to push those clients toward new dreams. Remember, clients usually know what they want but not what they need. As Dr. Sandeep K. Krishnan wrote in his book *The Mind of a Consultant,* "The important element that I have seen that firms look for in consultants is an ability to deeply understand the client first. But how does the client define success? Particularly when entering a new market case, you need a good understanding of the client."[1]

Sometimes the part of the presentation that you think is the best idea or solution for this particular project is shot down in a matter of seconds. Regroup mentally. Don't get married to your ideas.

Part of what constitutes a positive consultant mindset is approaching each project as if there are things to learn and ways to improve. A positive mindset also involves a clear sense of purpose, accompanied by a sound work ethic–as in, hard work. In addition, constantly build your network, which, in turn, can benefit your client.

Develop your own style and personal brand. There is not one single style that works better than the next. I have observed consultants who were somewhat introverted, yet they were able to communicate goals to the clients. For me, however, a key in achieving project success is in the area of presentational skills. A major role for the consultant is to teach.

The more effective the consultant is as a communicator, the better goals and objectives can be achieved—and more dreams can be interpreted well. Build your credibility. This comes with experience. The testimonial of your previous clients helps, as will your writing and presentations. Your last project is important, but so are the previous ones. Draft a list of the "best of," and try to capture key elements of each project that stand out in specific areas: "It was in this newspaper that we were able to change the team's mentality from print to digital" or "After we designed a new navigational system, traffic increased over 30 percent for this client's website." Sometimes it is changes in the team's makeup that are the highlight of a project.

In *The Mind of a Consultant,* Dr. Sandeep K. Krishnan mentions two words that represent what should be the essential mindset for an effective consultant: "Be yourself." [2]

Consultant Margarita Moreno agrees that for a consultant's mindset, "The best consultants learn from their clients and add to the great ideas or 'nuggets' being presented by the client. A consultant who does not grow or adapt is a 'one trick pony' and won't survive. A consultant also recognizes his/her limits. A consultant is never scared to bring in someone with expertise. A consultant has a voracious appetite for learning and for getting better in his/her field every day. A consultant believes that good ideas come from anywhere—even if it's just the inspiration of an idea that can grow into a better idea." [3]

🔅💡 CALM DOWN
An Adaptable Mindset Is Key

Successful consultants are prepared to shift gears, change strategy, edit the presentation, and be ready to listen. The mindset of a good consultant involves the following traits: adaptability and flexibility, empathy and emotional intelligence, analytical and critical thinking, resilience and persistence, and continuous learning and curiosity. Most important: a positive attitude and the ability to listen.

THE IMPORTANCE OF CULTURE (CONSULTING ABROAD).

Dr. Sandeep Krishnan, in *The Mind of a Consultant,* says, "How can onebuild cultural competencies to work across boundaries? First, by understanding that we, as groups of people, differ from one another. Secondly, by understanding that this difference is the concept for something beautiful, where we can learn from each other and use different approaches depending on the shifting contexts."[4]

The consultant's radar needs to be on for the cultural nuances that become important when working with people with backgrounds distinctly different from that of the consultant. My lessons in this area were learned firsthand.

After years of cutting my consulting teeth with small projects, many of them in upstate New York and other US states, with medium to low circulation dailies and weeklies, an opportunity to go abroad appeared. I already knew that each individual newsroom has a culture that is unique and different. Now it was time to learn about the more real cultural differences that come when you get a stamp on your passport and enter a foreign country. For me, that first consultation abroad was in Argentina—the land of the *tango* and some of the best wines in the world.

It was the end of my session on newspaper layout and design at the **American Press Institute,** in May 1980. The young man approaching me was Federico Massot, whose family owned **La Nueva Provincia,** a Latin American company (in Buenos Aires) and where I went on to work on several other dailies. That was the start of my love affair with Argentina, and especially its capital, Buenos Aires, which still ranks among my forever five favorite cities in the world (the others are Madrid, Paris, Stockholm, and Cape Town).

La Nueva Provincia was my first project outside of the United States, the start of an incredibly exciting career as a global consultant. It was here that I learned to respect culture, history, brand, and all that is there long before any of us arrives to keep the publication's "constant evolution" in motion. Respecting the richness of the past is key.

The question of culture has always been at the forefront of my thinking. I am a bicultural, bilingual person. In a way, this sets in motion tons of behaviors that I apply unconsciously to everything I do, from how I make personal decisions, to the language I dream in—I dream in English, but when conversing with my parents or grandparents, my brain switches to Spanish.

CULTURES ARE RICH IN UNIQUENESS.
From time to time, someone will ask me: "Mario, you were born in Cuba, came to America as a young teenager, and have lived most of your life as an American, but you travel the world—which culture defines you? Do you feel more Cuban? More American?"

Sometimes I feel like a citizen of the world, and it is not a bad thing. Today, the world is our neighborhood, and fast, immediate communication and access to information make that neighborhood a smaller village all the time. But back to the question of culture and identification. I guess I am a bicultural person most of the time, with moments in which I feel extremely Cuban—like when I smell a good picadillo or am in the presence of a great artisanal Cuban dessert, like toronja en conserva, not to mention when I hear Cuban music, when both feet are 150 percent Cuban each. This comes naturally and enriches my life.

Then, of course, I love America, my adopted homeland that took us in as refugees, something one never forgets. I love everything about America, especially my American children and grandchildren, but also a good Macy's Thanksgiving Day Parade, the Fourth of July fireworks, the sense of optimism and constant renewal that is the foundation of who we are as Americans—even in the worst of times.

I put my hand on my heart to recite the Pledge of Allegiance, and, if abroad, my eyes get misty when I hear the "Star-Spangled Banner." I am sentimentally patriotic for the US, which I consider my country, and symbolically and culturally attached to all things Cuban, especially the music, art, literature, and food. That makes me a typical bicultural person. There are many of us around the world: true to our roots but devoted and patriotic about our adopted land.

With my sense of being a proud Cuban, I honor not just the land where I was born but also the memory of my parents, who were 100 percent true, patriotic Cubans until the very end. With my sense of respect, gratitude, and patriotism for my adopted land, the US, I am a walking example that the American dream is possible, and I hope to pass all of those feelings to my eleven grandchildren, who have become part of the great American melting pot.

THE CONSULTANT, WORK, AND CULTURE.
Then comes the culture of work. I have worked in 122 countries in six continents to date. With each project, in each new country, I learned enormously about the impact and influence that culture has in the way we talk, think, and carry out our professional duties. An element of sustainability for me, after fifty-five years in this business, has been to respect each of the cultures I encounter in my work.

It was clear to me from that first trip to Argentina, in the late 1970s, to work with **La Nueva Provincia,** in Bahia Blanca, my first project outside the United States, that the first step in succeeding as a consultant in a foreign land was to show respect for how others think—by the way, one does not have to leave the country or deal with a different culture to do that. Especially if one is an American consultant, one must avoid imposing views that others may consider to have an "air of American superiority complex." The first step for me in each engagement is to listen and to acquaint myself with the people and their culture.

As a runner for years and now a power walk enthusiast, I go out early in the morning through every city in which I work. I observe my surroundings, how people decorate their windows, the colors they paint the outside of their houses, even what they throw in their trash. How they treat their animals. How they advertise consumer goods in the streets. How they assemble or follow traffic signs. All of this weaves the cloth that I sort of wrap myself in to deal with the project at hand. Once inside the organization, I try to think as if I were a permanent part of this culture.

WHAT WORKS IN ONE COUNTRY MAY NOT IN ANOTHER.
The global consultant must look carefully at the stamps on his passport and change gears when working in different countries. One cannot transfer a design model from Brazil to Scandinavia. Some ideas may be universal (navigation, legibility, clarity), but others vary distinctively (color, typography, and, most importantly, a newspaper's look and feel, which I have come to realize varies from country to country). There is no such thing as a "newspaper look" that fits all. The same applies to business models and strategies.

What may be a classic newspaper look in one place constitutes a boring, "don't go there" type of newspaper in another place. What may be loud Carmen Miranda colors for one newspaper in Stockholm are exactly the colors the doctor ordered for that newspaper in Fortaleza.

Appeal to the senses is important when one studies the likes or dislikes of a culture. I have always thought that the moment one steps out of an aircraft and walks the plank down to the baggage claim, one smells the country. Have you experienced this? If you disembark in Delhi, the first aroma of India embraces you in a welcome, but when you do the same in Buenos Aires, it is a totally different smell, as is Copenhagen or Moscow. I usually let my senses capture the culture, visually and otherwise. But I am also aware of two important things:

1. Those with whom I am working are sizing me up for what they perceive to be my cultural background, just as I am doing with them. (Don't be the ugly American!)

2. I must be true to my cultural values without sacrificing them as I respect those of the people with whom I work.

On item number one—pay attention to style—I always get a kick out of the way my German or Scandinavian clients, for example, always see me as an exotic bird. Indeed, I may be one, and that is okay with me. To the more reserved Nordic cultures, a person who, like me, talks with his hands, moves constantly during a presentation, never reads from a script, and ad-libs along the way, reacting to the mood of the moment and the audience (blame this on my childhood acting days in Cuba?) is, indeed, an exotic breed. The fact that I insist on being referred to informally as Mario, as opposed to Dr. García (it is always most troublesome to get them to do that in Austria, for some reason), and that I talk to everyone the same way, from the CEO and owner to the lady who brings me coffee and water, is something many find strange. And often a foreign client will tell me, in flattering tones: "Well, Mario, you live in the US, but you are not a typical American."

A typical American—what is that? I smile, knowing they are trying to tell me something nice, and I never open the Pandora's box to ask: What is a typical American? Some questions are meant to linger.

In Latin America, however, my clients always tell me: "You think like a Yankee." Why do I think like a Yankee? Because I insist on punctuality, following deadlines, and the American work ethic. As one Colombian editor put it to me: "Mario, you are packaged like a Cuban with the head of an American." Talk about picturesque language with a cultural twist. It is not all roses and flattering statements, though; no, sir.

As already mentioned, **Die Zeit,** Germany's intellectual weekly, remains my most difficult project to date. Why? The German editors thought an American could never understand German culture.

It was a wake-up call for me. Perhaps I had not understood German culture as well as I should. So I immersed myself in a learning process. At times, perceptions of culture get in the way of moving on with a project or in the aftermath of the project, as was the case with **The Journal**. It was 2001, and we were granting a lot of interviews to launch the new look of **The Journal.** Repeatedly, reporters would latch on to the connection between a former refugee who had arrived in the US as a child escaping communism now redesigning the ultimate tool of American capitalism. At first it was fun to talk about it, but eventually, it kept me from talking about the real changes in the design of the newspaper and how it would be easier to navigate it. In this case, culture "comparisons" appeared more interesting to many reporters than the story at hand: the visual change of **The Journal.**

I must admit that at moments like that, you feel like your cultural background is a heavy suitcase, and you wish the airline would lose it for two or three days, as happens with my real suitcases at least twice a year.

Fortunately, we are what we are, the total result of our cultural backgrounds, and we carry the culture suitcase wherever we go.

Mine is a little heavier because it carries two solid cultures that are part of me and of which I am proud, plus the goodies and the essence of the many cultures that I have come to admire and embrace during the past fifty-five years. A frame that hangs in my Florida home captures it best: I am a better person having seen the sun rise on the other side of the world. I am thankful for the opportunities consulting presented.

WHEN IN RUSSIA . . .
In 2019, I happened to be invited to help a group of Russian editors with the launch of **Moscovskiye Novosti,** the iconic Russian weekly that would now reappear as a daily. This was interesting, since the two cultural entities that I represent—American and Cuban—pose a bit of a handicap with some Russians, though not all. As an American consultant, I am perceived with the doubtful eye that is cast on anything America, the sort of "we love you and we hate you" attitude that may date back to the days of the Cold War and the USSR. But, oh, the Cuban connection isn't so good either. I decided to wear my citizen of the world hat here.

There are some in Russia old enough to remember when the Soviets made Cuba their second home, and that meant sending funds and goodies to the Caribbean island, which the locals perceived as "taking it from us to give to Castro." So, better to be a citizen of the world here, evoking things from both of my cultures that generate smiles and positive reactions: American movies and Cuban mojitos. I stuck to the creation of the newspaper, which launched successfully. Sometimes the consultant walks on broken glass. Wear sturdy shoes. From my notes:

PERSONAL NOTE
When The Client Is Also a Key Influential Medium

Moscow, November 11, 2010—Yesterday we presented a brief history of **Moscovskiye Novosti** and the important and influential role it played since its arrival in 1980, pushing for an end to the Cold War and ushering in perestroika.

Now, a team of editors, reporters, and designers prepares to launch the legendary MN as a daily, planned for February 2011. The clock is ticking, and we are busy with meetings and plenty of hands-on workshops to design not just the printed newspaper but all platforms. As we get closer to agreeing on that important first step of "look and feel"—what readers will perceive from looking at the front page of the newspaper in ten seconds—we now devote most of the day today to a continuation of our discussions for the digital platforms, and the iPad app, of which I am the chief architect.

Of special interest: The new team of the MN, especially its digital division, is rather young. They were mere children when the Soviet Union collapsed and the new Russia emerged. They have grown up knowing the role that the MN played in the history of their country but were not readers of the newspaper; and, of course, there was no digital version of the MN when it started. (Epilogue: This newspaper ceased publication. **Moscovskiye Novosti's** acting editor in chief, Irakly Gachechiladze, in March 2014 told reporters: "The decision has been made to sell [Moskovskiye Novosti] to the Moscow authorities. The conditions of the deal are being agreed on." (5) In farewell postings dated April 24, 2014, the newspaper's staff told readers: "Everyone knows who's to blame, we know what to do . . . We're sorry to say goodbye to you indefinitely. Our site won't be updated for some time. But we hope that that time will be short and fly by! Until next time! We'll miss you, too!") •

Consultants must take into account elements of culture and, in this case, geopolitics that may have an effect on the overall progress and success of the project.

The World Is Your Neighborhood.

↳ **Santiago (Chile).**

↳ **Amsterdam (Netherlands).**

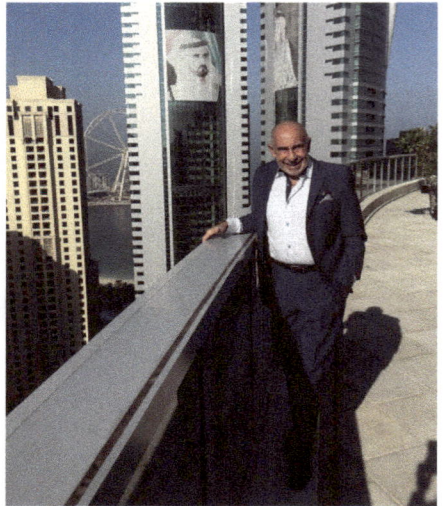
↳ **Dubai (United Arab Emirates).**

↳ **Here I blend with the sights of London (UK).**

↳ **Diaries are my travelogues.**

↳ **Las Palmas of Gran Canaria (Spain).**

↳ **Oslo (Norway).**

↳ **Bogotá (Colombia).**

↳ **Singapore.**

DIALOGUE
Beware the Client's Culture

Successful consulting requires a deep appreciation for and adaptation to the local culture. Listening and acclimating to the local environment and people is the first step in any engagement. Observing local customs, behaviors, and environments provides valuable insights. Consulting across different countries necessitates adaptability; what works in one region may not work in another. Consultants are also perceived through the lens of their cultural background, which influences interactions. Being open and flexible helps bridge cultural gaps and fosters better working relationships. Personal experiences and cultural ties significantly shape one's approach and philosophy in consulting. Cultural immersion is key—understanding local practices, from everyday life to professional norms, enhances consulting effectiveness.

Expertise

Part 3

Brand Yourself a Winner!

I n today's competitive landscape—across industries and disciplines—developing a personal brand is not a luxury but a necessity. For consultants in particular, the brand acts as a proxy, walking into the room before the individual does. It shapes first impressions, conveys trustworthiness, and distinguishes the consultant in a crowded marketplace. Branding is not just about recognition—it's about relevance and reputation. It defines you and describes your uniqueness.

The visual identity of a brand—logo, typography, color palette, and iconography—functions as a silent storyteller. Each design decision communicates intention: A serif font may suggest tradition and authority, while a bold sans-serif speaks to modernity and innovation. These elements are more than decorative; they are strategic. They must be clear, memorable, and emotionally resonant with the intended audience.

Effective branding often begins with the self. A consultant's name, heritage, and personal values can—and should—inform the branding process. In the case of **García Media**, for instance, the inclusion of the name García, the deliberate use of bright colors reflecting Hispanic identity, and even the accented í all contribute to a sense of cultural authenticity. This personal dimension not only distinguishes a brand —it makes it more relatable and human.

Brands are not static. They evolve alongside the professionals they represent. Whether due to changes in audience expectations, design trends, or strategic repositioning, updating visual elements such as logos or typefaces is a healthy part of brand maintenance. What matters is that these evolutions serve a purpose and remain aligned with the core identity and mission of the consultant or firm. Three principles should guide the creation of any personal brand identity:

- Simplicity ensures clarity and memorability.
- Relevance aligns the brand with the values and expectations of its audience. Sets one consultant apart from another.
- Uniqueness helps the brand stand apart in a crowded field.

Each element, from color choice to typeface, should serve these pillars to build a brand that is not only attractive but also strategically sound. Artificial intelligence is now a transformative ally in branding. From generating logo concepts to creating consistent, personalized content across platforms, AI empowers consultants to amplify their identity with scale and precision. Tools like **ChatGPT** can analyze audience data, refine messaging, and even script social media posts that align with the visual and tonal identity of the brand.

Consultants should not treat branding as an afterthought. Instead, it should be developed before their first client meeting or project pitch. A strong, coherent brand creates immediate credibility and helps generate what Alan Weiss calls "parachute business"–opportunities that land without solicitation, drawn by the gravitational pull of a well-known and respected brand. A strong brand says "you must hire me."

Branding Yourself

Regardless of what product or service one tries to sell, developing a brand is extremely important. The brand walks into the room before you do, thus the importance of logo and visual specifics that convey what the brand stands for. Those in charge of creating brand identities spend considerable time evaluating type fonts, color palettes, and the impacts of icons or illustrations. It is all time well spent. A well-developed brand helps consultants stand out, build trust, and attract clients.

When I first created my firm, I knew immediately that I wanted my name, García, included. It was not difficult in the late 1980s to realize that the word *media* should be a part of it too. Thus, **García Media** was born. We have changed our logo typography and style three times in the almost four decades that García Media has been in existence. There was always a good excuse to do so. The young people surrounding me would come to me and tell me that perhaps the time had come to update the brand. I am all for change, and having sat through many painful hours discussing brand logo changes with my clients, I did not want our own logo transformations to take much precious time from our projects. Bright colors have always been part of our **García Media** color palette. As a Hispanic, I identify with red, orange, and yellow.

Then would come the issue of whether to put an accent on the "i" in García, which is the correct form in Spanish. I said *sí* to that. Nice touch.

The visuals of your brand should be simple, remembering that less is best, and that people will make some conclusions about you and your brand from the moment they look at your logo.

THE PERSONAL BRAND AND HOW TO DEVELOP IT

Here are the three essentials that I recommend when creating your personal brand logo:

SIMPLICITY

· Clarity and memorability: A simple logo is easy to recognize and remember. It should avoid excessive details and complex elements that can clutter the design.

· I take pride in the number of publication logos that I helped to modernize and unclutter during my career as a design consultant. Gone are all those American eagles, flags, lakes, sunrises, and old sail boats, not to mention mascots.

RELEVANCE

· Target audience: If you are a consultant pitching your services to the 200 largest business firms in the world, chances are that your logo should appeal to a sophisticated audience of CEOs and marketing directors. Less is best, particularly for this crowd.

· Personal connection: The logo should reflect the personal brand's identity, values, and mission. It should communicate who you are and what you stand for, creating an immediate connection with your audience. For me, bright colors are a salute to my Hispanic heritage. For some, it is the type selection that reflects what you wish to convey. What part of you does your brand put forth?

UNIQUENESS

· Distinctiveness: The logo should stand out from competitors and be instantly recognizable as belonging to your personal brand. Avoid generic symbols and overused design trends. A good logo will be timeless. It communicates fast in a positive way.

• Developing your brand begins with the creation of a logo, but it also involves other areas where promotion of the brand is key. AI may be helpful with promoting the services of a consultant.

• AI-driven tools can help consultants create personalized content that aligns with their brand identity and resonates with their target audience. By analyzing audience data, AI can generate content that is relevant, timely, and engaging, ensuring consistent brand messaging across multiple platforms.

I recommend creating branding elements before you even pitch your first project. Your visual brand will evolve with your practice. Alan Weiss, a prominent consultant, speaker, and author renowned for his expertise in the consulting industry, has said this about the importance of branding yourself: "When you achieve a significant brand, you'll be the beneficiary of what I call 'parachute business,' which is a business that 'drops in.'"[1]

THE ROLE OF AI IN DEVELOPING A CONSULTANT'S BRAND.
In the contemporary consulting landscape, the importance of personal branding cannot be overstated. A well-developed brand helps consultants stand out, build trust, and attract clients.

AI is emerging as a powerful tool that can assist consultants in creating and enhancing their brand. Prompt your AI bot with specific details.

How to Use AI Tools to Create Branding Content

Begin with good prompting, as in this example: "You are a marketing expert, and you will assist me to promote my consulting services. We at **García Media** offer services in a variety of areas: coaching and training for mobile storytelling, introduction to AI and prompt engineering workshops, newsroom transformation, design across platforms: mobile, websites, print products. Offer me samples of text we can use for social media promotions, and suggest visuals."

Chat GPT response:
Here are some sample texts and visual suggestions for promoting García Media's consulting services on social media:

Mobile Storytelling Coaching and Training
Text: "Unlock the power of mobile storytelling with **García Media**! Join our expert-led coaching sessions to transform your storytelling skills and engage your audience like never before. *#MobileStorytelling #MediaTraining #GarciaMedia*"

"Ready to captivate your audience with compelling stories? Our mobile storytelling training at García Media will equip you with the skills you need. Sign up today! *#Storytelling #MobileFirst #GarciaMedia*"

"Transform your narrative with mobile-first storytelling techniques. Enroll in our training program and master the art of engaging content creation. *#ContentCreation #MobileStorytelling #GarciaMedia*"

Visuals: Images of interactive workshops with participants engaged in mobile storytelling activities. Before-and-after examples of stories transformed by mobile storytelling techniques. Infographics highlighting the benefits of mobile storytelling.

Artificial Intelligence and Prompt Engineering Workshops

Text: "Step into the future of media with our AI and prompt engineering workshops. Learn how to leverage AI to enhance your content creation process. *#AIWorkshops #PromptEngineering #GarciaMedia"*

"Empower your newsroom with the latest in AI technology. Our workshops cover everything from AI basics to advanced prompt engineering. *#ArtificialIntelligence #MediaInnovation #GarciaMedia"*

"Discover the potential of AI in the media. Join our workshops to learn how prompt engineering can revolutionize your content creation. *#AI #PromptEngineering #GarciaMedia"*

Visuals: Images of participants engaged in AI and prompt engineering activities. Diagrams showing the integration of AI in media workflows. Quotes and testimonials from past workshop attendees.

Newsroom Transformation

Text: "Transform your newsroom with García Media's expert consulting. Embrace the digital age and enhance your workflow efficiency. *#NewsroomTransformation #DigitalMedia #GarciaMedia"*

"Ready for a newsroom revolution? Our consulting services help you adapt to the changing media landscape. *#NewsroomConsulting #MediaTransformation #GarciaMedia"*

AI can monitor online mentions, reviews, and sentiment about a consultant's brand, providing real-time insights into their reputation. By using AI-powered reputation management tools, consultants can promptly address negative feedback, highlight positive testimonials, and maintain a positive brand image.

AI analytics can provide deep insights into market trends, audience preferences, and competitive landscapes. Consultants can leverage these insights to develop data-driven personal branding strategies that position them as thought leaders and experts in their field.

PERSONALIZED CONTENT CREATION AND DISTRIBUTION.
AI-driven tools can help consultants create personalized content that aligns with their brand identity and resonates with their target audience. By analyzing audience data, AI can generate content that is relevant, timely, and engaging, ensuring consistent brand messaging across multiple platforms. Most importantly, the voice and key personality traits of the consultant should be reflected in the brand.

ENHANCED SOCIAL MEDIA PRESENCE AND ENGAGEMENT.
AI tools can optimize social media strategies by analyzing trends, monitoring engagement, and automating posts. This enables consultants to maintain an active and consistent presence on social media, engage with their audience effectively, and build a strong online brand.

Example: Hootsuite's AI-powered analytics help consultants schedule posts, track performance, and engage with followers, ensuring a robust and dynamic social media presence. (2) So, if you gave a presentation at a well-known organization's annual gathering, you can post highlights of the presentation on your blog or social media, or see which participants have posted about your presentation, then you repost those testimonials.

ADVANCED REPUTATION MANAGEMENT.
AI can monitor online mentions, reviews, and sentiment about a consultant's brand, providing real-time insights into his reputation. By using AI-powered reputation management tools, consultants can promptly address negative feedback, highlight positive testimonials, and maintain a positive brand image.

Example: Brand24 uses AI to track online mentions and analyze sentiment, helping consultants manage their reputation by responding to feedback and engaging with their audience. (3)

DATA-DRIVEN PERSONAL BRANDING STRATEGIES.
AI analytics can provide deep insights into market trends, audience preferences, and competitive landscapes. Consultants can leverage these insights to develop data-driven personal branding strategies that position them as thought leaders and experts in their field.

ENHANCED CLIENT INTERACTION AND PERSONALIZATION.
AI-driven chatbots and virtual assistants can provide personalized interactions with potential clients, offering instant responses and valuable information. This not only enhances the client experience but also positions the consultant as accessible and technologically adept.

By leveraging AI for personalized content creation, social media engagement, reputation management, data-driven strategies, and client interaction, consultants can establish themselves as authoritative and trusted figures in their industry. The five key contributions discussed— personalized content, enhanced social media presence, advanced reputation management, data-driven strategies, and enhanced client interaction—highlight the transformative potential of AI in personal branding. As AI continues to evolve, its role in shaping the future of consulting and personal branding will become increasingly significant, necessitating a strategic and proactive approach to its adoption.

In his podcast, The Consulting Success Podcast, [4] host Michael Zipursky features interviews with successful consultants who share their insights and experiences. He has two recommendations for successful consultants to promote their brand:

• Networking: Leverage your network to build relationships
and uncover new business opportunities.

• Online presence: Maintain a strong online presence through
a professional website and social media, and use search engine
optimization to attract potential clients. My blog is responsible for
bringing me a variety of clients.

THE CONSULTANT AS PRESENTER.
The best branding strategies for the consultant are presentations. I make an effort to gain visibility via speaking engagements in a variety of organizations where potential media clients may attend, from international conferences to the more regional and even local ones.

This requires that the consultant learn the basic skills of putting presentations together, something which today's technology has made so much easier. Today, a variety of software, such as PowerPoint and Keynote, among others, can help you craft a great presentation that is easy to edit and project onto the screen.

Gone are the days of slide carousels and having to photograph images to be turned into slides. Today, I find myself able to edit a presentation mere minutes before giving it. The following tips will help you to prepare presentations that inform and impress:

• Make the presentation just about the right length: thirty to forty-five minutes is best.

• Engage your audience with the first few images: Start with a compelling story, a surprising fact, or a thought-provoking question to grab attention. Make everyone in the audience feel as if this presentation is specifically crafted for her.

• Adapt your message to the specific audience: Insist that your conference organizer send you a list of attendees ahead of time so that you can get an idea of who is in the audience, their specific roles within their organizations, etc. As a media consultant, I always like to "localize" my presentation to offer comments about the audience's output. Understand their interests, challenges, and the industry context. Include relevant case studies or examples that resonate with them.

• Tell the audience what you are going to cover: This helps the audience follow along and sets clear expectations. Ensure your points are logically sequenced. Use transitions to guide the audience from one section to the next. I usually like to have three or four major "baskets" of topics and tell the audience at the start what these are going to be. For example: transformation, storytelling, knowing your audience, and design.

• Keep visual continuity throughout: Use high-resolution images, infographics, and videos. Avoid cluttered slides; keep text minimal. Maintain a consistent design theme with your branding. Use your brand colors, fonts, and logo. There must be a consistent visual language throughout. Remember, less is best. Or as a design director in one of my workshops once told his team of designers: "Don't wear all your jewelry to the prom."

• Body language and voice modulation are important: Maintain good posture, make eye contact, and use hand gestures to emphasize points. Vary your pitch, tone, and pace to maintain interest. Avoid a monotone delivery. If possible, let the images in the presentation guide you, and avoid reading from a script in front of you. The tone should be one of talking to fellow colleagues, not that of a professor giving a lecture to a freshman class in a large auditorium.

• Allow for audience engagement/participation: Ask questions, invite comments, and encourage participation. Acknowledge responses and build on them. Be flexible and adapt your delivery based on audience reactions. While opinions vary on this, I favor questions throughout the presentation. I tell the audience at the start: "Raise your hand if you have a question during the presentation so that you don't forget a question referring to a specific image." But, of course, it is often left to the conference organizers to develop a policy on questions. The majority prefer scheduled Q&A at the end of the presentation.

• Recap key takeaways at the end of the presentation: Recap the main points of your presentation. Reinforce key takeaways. Provide clear next steps or actions for your audience. Invite them to connect with you for further discussion. My last two slides always offer the key takeaways from the presentation, then one where I express my gratitude to the audience and provide contact information and a QR code.

• Budget enough time to stay at the venue of the presentation: Normally, many people who are too shy to ask questions in the audience will want to come and speak to you individually. Keep your business cards handy.

• What program to use for your presentation: PowerPoint and Keynote are both robust options with a variety of templates and design tools. Keep slides clean and professional.

• Just in case: Always have a backup of your presentation on a USB drive and in the cloud. Be prepared for technical difficulties and know how to troubleshoot them. Of course, when all else fails, be ready to speak without any visuals. I remember I was once scheduled to give a presentation about color, and the visuals did not work. How do you explain a color palette without anything on the screen? I reached for my tie, showed my socks, and emphasized the hue color of my shirt that day. Since that day, I often remind my students about to give a presentation that if the technology fails, simply "reach for the tie."

• Follow-ups: I always make notes of those who expressed an interest in my consulting services and contact them via email soon after the event: just a simple note to say that it was a pleasure to meet them and to offer to answer any questions they may have about my presentation and/or services.

IT'S ALL RIGHT TO HAVE BUTTERFLIES IN YOUR STOMACH.
Not everyone enjoys public speaking. I have known many excellent consultants, experts in their field, who admitted that getting up in front of a group was a stressful experience. While I can understand that not everyone is trained as an actor, I also know that successful consultants are good at presenting their ideas in front of a group.

To claim differently would be dishonest. However, regardless of how many times you appear in front of an audience–and many theater actors agree–sometimes those few minutes before you appear in front of an audience can put butterflies in your stomach. That's normal.

These are butterflies that remind you that you are nervous and tense about whatever the business at hand is: a first date, a job interview, that first briefing meeting on a new project, or, in my case, a presentation before fifty or five hundred.

There is nothing to be ashamed of when those butterflies appear. No matter how many decades I have been doing this, or after hundreds (maybe thousands?) of presentations, there is always that butterfly that lands in the center of my stomach perhaps five minutes before my session begins. In my case, it dissipates quickly–the butterfly flies away the moment I utter the first line and see the audience. The fun begins then.

In fact, butterflies in your stomach can lead to better preparation and a more focused approach and are a reminder that success is not necessarily guaranteed by experience and even superb preparation.

People often tell me that I don't appear to have any concerns about taking to the stage to do a presentation. Of course, I have practice, and I sometimes do a presentation per day for different audiences. Nerves? Not at all. It could be that I started as a child actor at the age of eight in my native Cuba, for which I am thankful, as it prepared me for the stage and for audiences.

The same applies to projects: After having completed hundreds of projects, I always get a butterfly or two in my stomach when faced with the task of starting a new project. Will I be able to grasp the essence of the project? Of what the managers want to accomplish?

Will I create something that has a positive effect on the audience? Will I be able to interpret the client's dream properly? Those butterflies guarantee that you are on your toes, that you pay attention, and that you listen to the briefing. Butterflies are a magnificent guarantee that you don't rest on your laurels, a reminder that perhaps you need to go back and prepare some more, or that you are as vulnerable to circumstances as the next guy. Those butterflies don't disappear with experience.

I value my butterflies. My butterflies do not render me incapacitated–instead, they prompt me to stand at attention. I don't let them reside at the center of my stomach for too long, but I welcome their ephemeral presence.

They make me improve what I do, no matter how many times I have done it, and guarantee that I will remain at the top of my game.

Welcome, butterflies.

66 *Though butterflies in your stomach before a presentation may seem unsettling, I embrace them as vivid reminders to prepare thoroughly, strive for excellence, and never take the moment for granted."*

THE CONSULTANT ADAPTS QUICKLY.

I remind all members of my team that they must be flexible in a variety of areas, the biggest of which is calendar changes. These are frequent, as clients tend to fantasize about how quickly things can happen with their teams. Even the most precise Swiss and German clients have been forced to push dates of implementation.

If it can happen, it will happen: technological glitches and delays (the usual culprit), personnel changes (second reason for delays), project goal changes in mid-flight (these are difficult to handle!).

While some consultants specify how their professional fee changes if there are dramatic changes in the middle of the project, I have personally never used this practice. As a consultant, one must adopt agile methodologies to stay flexible and responsive to client needs. This approach allows for iterative development and continuous feedback, which improves the quality and relevance of solutions. Knowing this, the consultant can pace his own project tracking, knowing that most of the implementation dates will change.

I have never said no to a potential client for fear that his project will compete with time for another. Delays will happen. Timelines will be altered. Sometimes a psychic intervenes, and the implementation date is moved, as happened to me with a project in which the CEO's psychic simply told him: October will not be a good month to introduce the new product. The CEO agreed and told me so. We launched in November. The psychic was right, but, more importantly, it gave the content management system team extra weeks. All's well that ends well.

THE CONSULTANT AND PROJECT TRACKING.

The consultant does not need a psychic to tell her too many projects going simultaneously may not lead to good results. Pace yourself as you take on new clients. Be flexible but also know the number of clients you can serve well, how many trips you can take in a given month, and how many places you can be at the same time.

With so much of the work conducted remotely today, don't lose track of the simple fact of participation: Whether you are traveling to an office in Hong Kong or Chicago or sitting at your dining room table to face a client on a video call, it is you who must perform, be alert, be wise, be the expert. Rarely a week goes by when I don't do my simple project-tracking exercise: Write down the project titles, evaluate where each is in the process you have planned, and forecast yourself to four weeks from today and also three months from today. That should give you an idea of what new projects you can accept.

That's where the wise phrase "The Law of Raspberry Jam" comes in handy. That comes from *The Secrets of Consulting: A Guide to Giving and Getting Advice Successfully* by Gerald M. Weinberg, which offers practical wisdom and humorous insights into the art of consulting.

What is "The Law of Raspberry Jam"? Spread yourself too thin and lose impact: "The wider you spread it, the thinner it gets."[5]

This principle suggests that consultants should focus their efforts rather than spreading themselves too thin. Specializing and concentrating on specific areas can lead to more impactful and effective consulting. Indeed, focus and remind yourself and your clients that you are not an expert on everything, but where you are an expert, you are the best.

WRITE A BOOK.
After years of consulting, many consultants will admit to their friends that "I could write a book." The great American poet and novelist Sylvia Plath once said that "everything in life is writable about if you have the outgoing guts to do it, and the imagination to improvise." [6] Plath added that the worst enemy to creativity is self-doubt.

These are words that have resonated with me through the years and should be the same with other consultants reading this book. I don't think one is ever truly ready to write a book. In many cases, if you wait until you feel you are ready to write that book, it won't happen.

Those who wait till they are "ready" probably reach their end without ever writing it. Perhaps I should have waited a little longer to write each of my books. If so, some of the spontaneity that I now see in those texts would not be there. Perhaps we become more guarded with age.

The basis of book writing consists of a simple formula: One has a desire to share knowledge (or, in the case of fiction writers, to tell a story) one is passionate about. Although there are always others who may know much more about a subject than you, they may not necessarily be interested in writing the definitive book on the subject, so you focus on getting your own views out there, writing as fast as you can, and letting your writing start the dialogue—which usually happens quickly after the book is published.

HOW MY FIRST BIG BOOK HAPPENED.
The incredibly long, frigid, and snowy winters of Syracuse were conducive to taking the stairs of our two-story home on Sheatree Lane and typing away in the spare guest room that served as my home office. I would type two or three pages, then pause to look outside the window at the white stuff falling in slow motion. That first book would become **Contemporary Newspaper Design**, initially published in 1978. I was the young professor of graphic arts at Syracuse University's S.I. Newhouse School of Public Communications, and I truly could not find a good book to use in my Newspaper Design class. What began as a series of lectures during my first year teaching the course eventually developed into more of a book. I was blessed with many friends in the industry who contributed material. Like me, they were young and pioneering in a subject now referred to as "newspaper design" but which was treated more like "newspaper makeup or layout" in all of the literature of the time.

It was not an easy process, but eventually, Prentice Hall published the book. When I first sent out a prospectus about my "potential book," along with a table of contents, the reply was swift and direct, and I will always remember the impact it had on me:

"Dear Sir, thanks for sending us your book proposal, but there are only three colleges and universities in the country that offer a course for which your book might be adopted."

No, I was not surprised about this detail. But not one to give up easily, I engaged the help of publisher friends in the industry, many of whom told me their newsroom would buy two to four copies of that textbook. I informed Prentice Hall about that, and a contract arrived at my SU office. The book was eventually printed in three different editions, including a Spanish one, published through the University of Navarra, in Pamplona, Spain, under the title **Diseño y Remodelación de Diarios**.

These were not merely updates for each edition. In fact, I would almost rewrite the entire book since things were happening quickly, and the world of newspaper design probably had its fastest development and most far-reaching impact during the 1980s and early 1990s. Design went from a whim that a rare publisher or editor pursued to a necessary part of the storytelling process. This new text was needed. Sometimes you become aware of a resource that would enrich the work of people in that field, so you just create it yourself.

MAKE A NOTE
The Importance of Branding Yourself

The brand makes an impression before personal interaction. A logo and visual elements convey the brand's values and identity. Effective visual branding requires careful consideration of type fonts, color palettes, and icons, emphasizing simplicity and clarity to ensure recognition and memorability. Staying attuned to contemporary design trends and the input of younger team members can drive timely and effective brand updates. A simple logo is more likely to be recognized and remembered. It should avoid unnecessary details that could clutter the design. A distinctive logo helps the brand stand out in a crowded market, avoiding generic symbols and overused trends. Creating a timeless and unique brand identity ensures long-term recognition and differentiates the brand from competitors. Incorporate that branding element into presentations. Presentations, articles, and books are important to establishing and sustaining a brand as a consultant.

Artificial Intelligence and the Consultant

I n his informative book *Co-Intelligence: Living and Working with AI,* Ethan Mollick, a professor of management at Wharton School of the University of Pennsylvania, offers a panoramic but also detailed view of AI, with segments in which he describes AI as a person, a creative, a coworker, a tutor, and a coach.

A good consultant is all of these things too. And so it makes sense to look at AI for what it can offer us consultants as we assist clients with projects. Mollick writes that "AI excels at tasks that are intensely human. It can write, analyze, code and chat. It can play the role of marketer or consultant, increasing productivity by outsourcing mundane tasks . . ."[1] Mollick adds what we already know: AI systems also make mistakes, tell lies, and hallucinate answers, just like humans. Which is why the "human in the loop" concept is so important for anyone considering adapting AI to any type of work. Interesting phrase, "human in the loop."

Long before AI was part of our vocabulary, I had reassured my clients that I would be in the loop at all times during the entire project –to review, supervise, make corrections, and communicate with the in-house team. The "human in the loop" is part of the human/bot dance that is the foundation of my book **AI: The Next Revolution in Content Creation**. I wrote:

> AI can be of tremendous assistance to humans for a variety of tasks, but the process begins with human input, requires human supervision, and ends with human evaluation and amendment. This convergence of human ingenuity and artificial intelligence has the potential to redefine the role of content creators. AI holds a promise of revolutionizing the way we think, create, and share knowledge. It can analyze vast amounts of data, uncover hidden patterns, and generate novel ideas with efficiency. Yet, AI is ultimately a creation of the human intellect. AI can surprise us with its ability to provide information, but algorithms can't match a human's capacity for empathy, intuition, and moral judgment. The human spirit finds its truest expression in the realm of the subjective, the aesthetic, and the deeply emotional. AI is a long way from matching our creativity in the arts, literature, music, and other creative realms. AI can't yet replicate human essence. It's clear to me that this dynamic dance between AI and humans will yield brilliant and unpredictable results. At the moment, this dance is more like a waltz than a salsa, but the two principals are on the dance floor, getting to know each other's moves. [2]

A 2023 study led by Harvard Business School professors, in coordination with the Boston Consulting Group, found that consultants who worked with AI produced 40 percent higher quality results on eighteen different work tasks. A major takeaway from the study: "Our results show that this generation of LLMs are highly capable of causing significant increases in quality and productivity, or even completely automating some tasks, but the actual tasks that AI can do are surprising and not immediately obvious to individuals or even to producers of LLMs themselves.

"Because this frontier is expanding and changing, the overall results suggest that AI will have a large impact on work, one which will increase with LLM capabilities, but where the impacts occur will be uneven." [3]

As I sit writing a book about consulting, I wonder how AI could have helped me at those times when at the end of my consulting day, I would pour myself a glass of champagne and ponder how to face a challenge presented to me that day. In the spirit of what if, I prompted **ChatGPT** on a major challenge that I faced in Germany with the newspaper **Die Zeit.** The editors had told me that, as an American designer, I could not understand German elegance to be able to transmit it to my design concepts for their newspaper. If AI had been available to me back then, this would have been my approach:

Prompt: "You are Chango, a media consulting expert. You are going to help Mario García write a book chapter about consulting in which I wish to mention how AI could have helped me with a consulting challenge. This is an episode when a German client tells Mario: You can't do this project because as an American you can't ever know or understand German elegance. How can I learn about German elegance quickly? Your job is to offer unusual and interesting connections. You speak in an expert voice offering convincing arguments that will help Mario García understand German elegance."

ChatGPT: Certainly, Mario! Here's a segment that addresses the challenge posed by a German client questioning an American consultant's understanding of German elegance. This section aims to provide unusual and interesting connections to help you swiftly learn and demonstrate an appreciation for German elegance.

Chapter X: Bridging Cultural Gaps in Consulting by Understanding German Elegance: Beyond Stereotypes
When faced with the assertion that an American cannot understand German elegance, the key is to demonstrate a genuine commitment to learning and appreciating the cultural nuances that define elegance in Germany. Here are some strategies to quickly and effectively grasp the essence of German elegance:
Delving into Historical and Cultural Context
The Bauhaus Influence
German elegance is deeply rooted in the Bauhaus movement, which revolutionized design in the early 20th century. The Bauhaus philosophy emphasizes simplicity, functionality, and form following function. Understanding Bauhaus principles can provide a foundation for appreciating

German aesthetics in architecture, furniture, and graphic design.
Unusual Connection: Explore how the Bauhaus influence extends to modern German brands like Braun and Miele, which embody minimalist design and functionality. Analyzing their product designs can offer insights into contemporary interpretations of German elegance.

Classical Music and Literature

Germany's rich cultural heritage includes contributions from classical composers like Beethoven and Bach, as well as literary giants like Goethe and Schiller. These figures are synonymous with German elegance in the arts. Unusual Connection: Attend a performance at a renowned venue like the Berlin Philharmonic or read works by Thomas Mann. Experiencing these cultural touchstones firsthand can provide a deeper appreciation of the refined elegance embedded in German culture.

Engaging with Modern German Design and Fashion
Iconic Designers and Brands

German elegance today is also reflected in its fashion and design industries. Designers like Karl Lagerfeld and brands like Jil Sander are synonymous with sophisticated, understated elegance.
Unusual Connection: Study the design philosophies of contemporary German fashion designers. Visit flagship stores or exhibitions to observe how elegance is translated into modern clothing and accessories.

The Automotive Industry

Germany's automotive industry is a paragon of elegance and engineering excellence. Brands like Mercedes-Benz, BMW, and Audi are known for their sleek designs and meticulous craftsmanship.
Unusual Connection: Tour a German automotive factory or visit an auto show in Germany to see how precision and elegance are integrated into the manufacturing process. Understanding the design and production of these vehicles can offer unique insights into the broader cultural appreciation for elegance.

Immersing in Everyday German Life
Architectural Elegance

From the grandeur of Berlin's Reichstag to the modern elegance of the Elbphilharmonie in Hamburg, German architecture offers a blend of historical and contemporary elegance.

Unusual Connection: Take architectural walking tours in German cities to observe the integration of historical and modern elements. Engaging with local architects or guides can provide contextual insights into the design choices that define German elegance.

Culinary Experiences
German cuisine, often overlooked, has its own form of elegance, particularly in the presentation and flavors of regional specialties.

Unusual Connection: Dine at Michelin-starred restaurants in Germany, such as those in the Black Forest region. Pay attention to how culinary elegance is expressed through plating, ingredient selection, and service.

Building Credibility with German Clients
Demonstrating Respect and Curiosity
Show genuine respect for German culture and express a keen interest in learning from your clients. This approach can help bridge the initial gap and demonstrate your commitment to understanding their perspective.

Unusual Connection: Engage in cultural exchange activities such as cooking classes, art workshops, or local festivals. These experiences can provide a more intimate understanding of the subtleties of German elegance.

Collaborating with Local Experts
Partnering with local German experts or consultants can enhance your credibility and provide deeper insights into the cultural nuances.

Unusual Connection: Create a collaborative project that involves German designers, artists, or cultural historians. Their expertise can enrich your understanding and showcase a willingness to integrate local perspectives into your work.

Conclusion: Facing skepticism about your ability to understand and appreciate German elegance requires more than just surface-level knowledge. By delving into the historical, cultural, and modern expressions of elegance in Germany, you can build a robust understanding that resonates with your clients.

Demonstrating genuine curiosity, respect, and a willingness to immerse yourself in the nuances of German culture will not only bridge the cultural gap but also enhance your effectiveness as a consultant.

This segment provides a comprehensive approach to quickly learning about German elegance through unusual and interesting connections. It emphasizes the importance of cultural immersion, collaboration, and genuine curiosity in overcoming skepticism and building rapport with clients.

Or, I might have tried another version:

Prompt: In the realm of media consulting, understanding cultural nuances is paramount. I encountered a challenge with a German client who questioned my ability to grasp German elegance, stating, "You can't do this project because as an American, you can't ever know or understand German elegance."

Chat GPT: Certainly, Mario. Let's explore how AI could have assisted in navigating this challenge and provided a nuanced understanding of German elegance.

The Challenge of German Elegance. Leveraging AI for Cultural Insight
1. **AI-Powered Cultural Analysis:** AI has advanced significantly in understanding and analyzing cultural contexts. By utilizing AI tools like natural language processing (NLP) and machine learning, we can quickly gather and interpret vast amounts of data related to cultural aesthetics, preferences, and trends. Here's how AI could have helped:

Data Aggregation and Analysis: AI can
aggregate data from various sources, such as German fashion magazines, architectural journals, design blogs, and social media. By analyzing this data, AI can identify key themes, styles, and elements that define German elegance.
Semantic Analysis: NLP can perform a semantic analysis of texts, extracting insights on the connotations and subtle nuances associated with German elegance. This could involve understanding the language used in high-end German fashion, design, and cultural discussions.

2. AI-Driven Visual Insights:
Image Recognition and Analysis:
AI-driven image recognition tools can analyze thousands of images related to German design and fashion. These tools can highlight common patterns, color schemes, and design principles that epitomize German elegance.
Trend Analysis: Machine learning algorithms can identify emerging trends in German aesthetics by analyzing historical and contemporary visual data. This helps in understanding not only what is currently considered elegant but also the evolution of these standards over time.

3. AI as a Cultural Translator:
Cross-Cultural Communication Tools: AI-powered translation tools go beyond mere language translation. They can interpret cultural nuances and contextual meanings, offering deeper insights into how German elegance is perceived and articulated.
Virtual Assistants and Chatbots: Virtual assistants can simulate conversations with German designers, architects, and cultural experts, providing real-time feedback and insights into what constitutes German elegance.

4. Case Studies and Comparative Analysis:
Comparative Analysis Tools: AI can compare German elegance with other cultural standards of elegance, highlighting unique elements and differences. This comparative analysis can reveal the distinctive features of German elegance that might not be immediately apparent.
Case Study Generation: AI can generate case studies by analyzing successful German design projects across various fields, such as automotive design (e.g., Mercedes-Benz), fashion (e.g., Hugo Boss), and architecture (e.g., Bauhaus). These case studies can serve as references for understanding and applying the principles of German elegance.

Convincing Arguments for AI Utilization
Efficiency and Depth: AI provides a rapid, in-depth analysis that would take a human researcher months to achieve. This efficiency allows consultants to quickly bridge cultural gaps and offer informed recommendations.
Objective Insights: AI's data-driven approach ensures objectivity, minimizing personal biases and providing a balanced view of cultural aesthetics.

Innovative Solutions: By leveraging AI, consultants can offer innovative and unconventional solutions that resonate with cultural standards, thus demonstrating a deep understanding of the client's values.
Continual Learning: AI tools continuously learn and update their databases, ensuring that consultants have access to the latest trends and cultural insights, which is crucial for staying relevant and effective.

By integrating AI into the consulting process, we can transcend cultural barriers and demonstrate a profound understanding of concepts like German elegance. This not only enhances our credibility but also fosters stronger client relationships built on trust and respect for cultural authenticity. This approach underscores the transformative potential of AI in consulting, showcasing how technology can empower us to navigate complex cultural landscapes with finesse and precision.

NOT TOO BAD.
I would have welcomed this input. As chief architect of the project, or "the human in the loop," I would have been able to take inspiration from ChatGPT's outline and perhaps followed through with some of its suggestions, an advantage and inspiration I did not have when this occurred.

For example, the data aggregation of materials could have guided me promptly to specific references: fashion, automobiles, etc. Also important would have been utilizing AI's machine learning algorithms that can identify emerging trends in German aesthetics by analyzing historical and contemporary visual data. This helps in understanding not only what is currently considered elegant but also the evolution of these standards over time.

As it was, I did the research, slowly but in detail. Eventually we arrived at a prototype that reflected German elegance—and still does—but the process would have been faster and more efficient with AI serving as a coworker, a tutor, and a coach, as Mollick describes in his book.

Indeed, AI works as a well-oiled crane doing the heavy lifting and expediting the process for the consultant to hit the right target with the client. For today's consultant, trusting AI for collaborations—with the human in the loop and in control—means better results, more successful engagements with the project and the client, and an inspiration for initial thoughts that will be augmented when prompting AI for data and solutions.

I can anticipate AI serving as a great collaborator for consultants in every field—not substituting the consultant but enhancing his role and helping expedite processes. However, the benefits of AI as a coworker may be less for those consultants who are the most innovative.

AI NO HELP FOR MORE INNOVATIVE TYPES?
Researchers Anil Doshi and Oliver Hauser set out to study the causal impact of Generative AI (GenAI) on the production of a creative output in an online experiment where some writers could obtain ideas for a story from a GenAI platform.[4]

The boost in creativity primarily benefited writers who were least inherently creative, highlighting that the creativity humans contribute to a project remains superior. This serves as a reminder that, at least for now, humans are far from being obsolete.

Similarly, in another study by the National Bureau of Economic Research, access to AI tools increased productivity: a 34 percent improvement for novice and low-skilled workers but with minimal impact on experienced and highly skilled workers.[5] The future is about humans and AI collaborating effectively.

The study by Doshi and Hauser provides a nuanced understanding of how GenAI impacts creativity, highlighting the indispensable role of human ingenuity. For consultants, these insights can guide the effective integration of AI in creative processes, ensuring that technology serves to enhance, rather than diminish, the unique value that humans bring to the table. As we continue to explore the capabilities of AI, it is crucial to maintain a balanced perspective that celebrates and leverages the strengths of both human and AI.

THE HARVARD STUDY.
For many experimenting with artificial intelligence, a question that pops up constantly is "What can AI help me with?" What are those tasks in which AI becomes a sort of crane that can do the heavy lifting for me, and what are some tasks that my friend the bot is not ready to assist with—yet? A 2023 Harvard study titled *"Navigating the Jagged*

Technological Frontier: Field Experimental Evidence of the Effects of AI on Knowledge Worker Productivity and Quality" has gone deep into those questions. What I like about this study is that it was executed totally with consultants.

For doubters of AI's impact and benefit, the Harvard study emphasized that "in many industries and for many types of analytical tasks, the discussion is no longer about whether to adopt AI but rather about how to use AI." (6)

For this study, the preregistered experiment involved 758 consultants comprising about 7 percent of the individual contributor-level consultants with Boston Consulting Group. After establishing a performance baseline on a similar task, subjects were randomly assigned to one of three conditions: no AI access, GPT-4 AI access, or GPT-4 AI access with a prompt engineering overview: We suggest that the capabilities of AI create a "jagged technological frontier" where some tasks are easily done by AI, while others, though seemingly similar in difficulty level, are outside the current capability of AI, as in creative problem-solving.

For each one of a set of 18 realistic consulting tasks within the frontier of AI capabilities, consultants using AI were significantly more productive (they completed 12.2% more tasks on average, and completed tasks 25.1% more quickly), and produced significantly higher quality results (more than 40% higher quality compared to a control group).

Consultants across the skills distribution benefited significantly from having AI augmentation, with those below the average performance threshold increasing by 43% and those above increasing by 17% compared to their own scores. For a task selected to be outside the frontier, however, consultants using AI were 19 percentage points less likely to produce correct solutions compared to those without AI. Further, our analysis shows the emergence of two distinctive patterns of successful AI use by humans along a spectrum of human-AI integration. One set of consultants acted as "Centaurs," like the mythical half-horse/half-human creature, dividing and delegating their solution-creation activities to the AI or to themselves. Another set of consultants acted more like "Cyborgs," completely integrating their task flow with the AI and continually interacting with the technology. (7)

As we see in this study, AI can be a phenomenally helpful tool, but the more innovative and skilled humans still have the upper hand in creating work that is unique. Part of my work today is precisely about the value of the human—particularly in contrast to the output of artificial intelligence. In my classes and workshops, I refer to this as The Scent of the Human, then take it more specifically to various audiences, as in The Scent of the Writer and The Scent of the Artist. This concept captures the essence of what makes human-generated content feel authentic, emotionally resonant, and deeply personal. The Scent of the Human then emerges as a metaphor for what AI-generated work lacks.

In an age where machines can mimic tone and replicate structure, what remains most valuable is The Scent of the Human—the subtle signals of lived experience, perspective, and the emotional intelligence only a person can bring. The consultant is an expert, and, as Mollick asserts in his AI book: "The path to expertise requires a grounding in facts."(8)

AI also has facts. The Scent of the Consultant goes beyond facts and into lived experiences. Sophie Kahn, a digital artist and sculptor, speaks about the importance of "human error" or "gesture" in art. To err is human, goes the saying. Kahn emphasizes that what AI lacks is not capability but context. (9) In my own experiments with very creative artists, this is a theme that resonates. For consultants, it is drawing from the experience of a project long ago where one sees a glimpse of light that could illuminate the current project. We, as humans, have a body of lived experiences. They appear serendipitously, sometimes in a totally unrelated context. Humans can connect the disconnected.

Brian Christian, in his book *The Alignment Problem*, also delves into the philosophical distinctions between human and AI, pointing to the depth of "intentionality and subjectivity in human creativity." (10)

CAN AI REPLACE THE JOB OF THE CONSULTANT?

While many consultants embrace AI for how it can assist with a variety of tasks, and for its future potential, others fear what AI may do in terms of eliminating jobs for which consultants are currently hired.

For example, management consulting is on the list of jobs likely to get automated, according to consulting statistics provided by Runn. (11)

Will consultants be replaced by robots? To remain competitive and profitable, management consultants must increase productivity through automation. After decades of calls for a transformation, the management consulting industry is finally poised at the epicenter of disruption. The disruption of management consulting will affect clients, practitioners, and entire industries, from marketing to health care.

Some of the tasks that we consultants get hired to complete may, indeed, be taken over by AI. For example, data gathering, analysis, insight generation, risk assessment and mitigation, and automated report generation. Here the impact is major, as automated report generation significantly reduces the time and effort required to produce detailed reports, allowing consultants to focus on higher-value tasks such as strategic planning and client interaction. Next is project management and timeline optimization, since AI tools can streamline project management by optimizing timelines, resource allocation, and task scheduling. AI-driven project-management platforms can adjust plans in real time based on progress, unforeseen delays, or changes in project scope, leading to more efficient project execution, reducing costs and increasing the likelihood of meeting deadlines. AI can also provide early warnings about potential project bottlenecks or resource shortages, allowing for timely interventions.

Finally, AI can analyze sentiment and trends from social media platforms, news articles, and other public data sources. This analysis can provide insights into public perception, customer satisfaction, and emerging issues relevant to a client's business. By continuously monitoring and analyzing sentiment, consultants can offer clients real-time feedback on their brand, products, or services.

66 *The AI 'jagged frontier' arises because AI systems are designed with specific architectures, training data, and optimization goals that align with particular tasks, such as image recognition, but they are ill-suited for tasks such as understanding the sequence of events in a narrative."*

This can inform marketing strategies, crisis management, and customer engagement efforts, making them more responsive and adaptive to public opinion. By taking over tasks such as data analysis, risk assessment, report generation, project management, and sentiment analysis, AI enables consultants to focus on higher-level strategic thinking and client engagement.

Embracing AI-driven tools and methodologies will be essential for consultants to remain competitive and deliver superior value in a rapidly evolving market. And, still again, we see AI as a genius assistant, available 24/7 (never needs a day off), but which requires the human in the loop to verify accuracy. AI is the crane doing the heavy lifting; the human consultant takes advantage of AI but continues to be the chief architect of a project, perhaps with more time to devote to those tasks where only a human can provide what the client and the project require.

THE IMPORTANCE OF DEVELOPING AI SKILLS.

If the consultant is the human in the loop, regarding the use of AI as a collaborative element in a major consulting project, then it is imperative that the consultant develop a series of skills and competencies related to AI understanding and use, the most important of which is the way the human consultant communicates with the robots—or prompt engineering. The relationship between consultants and AI will be symbiotic, leveraging AI to enhance human capabilities while addressing complex business challenges. What are the skills a consultant of today must possess to make the most effective use of AI? You should be looking at areas like technical skills, data science and analytics, AI integration and implementation, analytical skills such as algorithmic understanding, and interpersonal skills such as communicating with AI specialists. With all this, we must also make ethical considerations about using AI.

TECHNICAL SKILLS.

The consultant today works right at the junction where personal expertise meets technology, the accelerating force of artificial intelligence, and the specific needs of each client. That's why technical skills—like understanding how AI works, how data drives decisions, and how to implement smart solutions—are no longer optional. They're part of the new toolbox every consultant must carry and include the following:

• **AI literacy and technical proficiency:** Consultants must have a strong understanding of AI technologies, including machine learning (ML), natural language processing (NLP), and computer vision. This involves not only knowing how these technologies work but also how to apply them effectively to solve business problems. In my workshops, I emphasize the importance of gaining knowledge of the essentials that make these bots our smart assistants. Think neural networks—AI robots mimic neural networks from human brains. Human brains process information through connectiveness, and AI is mimicking those processes.

• **Data science and analytics:** Proficiency in data science is crucial. Consultants will need to be skilled in data manipulation, statistical analysis, and the use of AI tools to extract insights from large datasets. Knowledge of programming languages like Python and R, as well as familiarity with AI frameworks such as TensorFlow and PyTorch, will be essential. [12] Not that you need to be an expert, but it helps to have some familiarity with those processes.

• **AI Integration and implementation:** Future consultants must be adept at integrating AI solutions into existing business processes. This includes understanding the technical requirements, ensuring compatibility with current systems, and managing the implementation process to minimize disruption and maximize efficiency. [13]

ANALYTICAL SKILLS.

The modern consultant is expected to harness the power of AI through predictive and prescriptive analytics forecasting future trends and offering actionable strategies rooted in data. Yet even the most advanced algorithms cannot replace the seasoned instinct, observation, and experience that often spark true insight, as in the understanding of human psychology.

In my own work in newspaper design, it was this human intuition that helped me anticipate transformative shifts—from the embrace of color to the rise of infographics. Equally vital is the ability to understand

and articulate how AI algorithms operate, ensuring that consultants can both trust their tools, like those I've listed, and translate complex outputs for nontechnical stakeholders.

• **Predictive and prescriptive analytics:** Consultants will need to go beyond descriptive analytics to provide predictive and prescriptive insights. This involves using AI to forecast future trends and recommend actionable strategies, thereby enabling clients to make informed decisions based on data-driven predictions. Of course, this does not substitute for the consultant's ability to combine instinct with observation and experience in predicting outcomes and trends. I often emerged from a specific project fully charged with ideas for having "discovered" what would become a trend. In my specific newspaper design field, I can think of such moments referring to the advent of color, use of white space, typographic trends, and use of infographics to help explain the news. The good consultant jumps ahead of the trends and connects the still disconnected.

• **Algorithmic understanding:** A deep understanding of how AI algorithms function is necessary to evaluate their performance, interpret their outputs, and explain these to nontechnical stakeholders. This skill helps in assessing the reliability and accuracy of AI-driven insights.

INTERPERSONAL SKILLS.
Interpersonal skills are the consultant's bridge to trust and collaboration. You will deal with diverse client personalities, the full spectrum of the human condition, plus different organizational cultures that require your empathy, active listening, and clear communication—often as critical as technical expertise. This is entirely infused with The Scent of the Human.

• **Communication of AI insights:** Effectively communicating complex AI concepts and insights to clients is critical. Consultants must be able to translate technical findings into clear, actionable business recommendations that stakeholders can understand and implement. AI tools can be ideal for summarizing and explaining.

• **Collaboration with AI specialists:** Working closely with AI experts, data scientists, and engineers will be a routine part of a consultant's job. Building strong interdisciplinary teams and fostering effective collaboration are essential for the successful deployment of AI projects. Presently, I make it a point to identify the role of AI for the company I am consulting with, then on the first day on the job, I establish communication with the AI- initiative team, knowing well that no project today can ignore the potential of AI. If there is no AI representation, then I urge the managers to go shopping for AI expertise in-house.

ADAPTIVE SKILLS

To thrive in an AI-powered consulting environment, professionals must commit to continuous learning while embracing a leadership role in promoting ethical AI use—balancing technical fluency with human oversight and responsibility.

• **Continuous learning:** The field of AI is rapidly evolving, so continuous learning and staying updated with the latest advancements in AI technology are crucial. Continuous learning includes participating in professional development programs, attending industry conferences, and engaging with academic research. AI is in its infancy, but already a formidable library of books, articles, and podcasts cover the basics and beyond. Still, engaging with AI is similar to learning to play the piano:
Daily practice makes it best. I surprise my grandchildren when I tell them that I chat with my bots a minimum of thirty-five minutes each day.

• **Ethical AI practices:** Consultants must understand and implement ethical AI practices. This involves ensuring AI systems are transparent, fair, and free from bias and that they comply with relevant regulations and ethical standards. Consultants will need to guide clients in responsible AI usage, addressing issues related to privacy, security, and societal impact. This is the one area where it is imperative that humans be alert and in the loop.

Ensuring that humans remain "in the loop" in processes involving AI, especially in vetting information, is critical. AI may misinterpret questions, provide incorrect data, or hallucinate entirely false information. Also, if the training data is biased, the AI might produce outputs that reflect or amplify those biases. Humans are necessary to identify and mitigate these ethical issues. Continuous human involvement also fosters accountability and trust in AI systems.

By 2029, the relationship between consultants and AI will be characterized by a high degree of collaboration and mutual enhancement. AI will serve as an augmentation tool, enhancing consultants' decision-making processes. AI systems will analyze vast amounts of data at unprecedented speeds, providing consultants with deeper insights and more accurate predictions. This allows consultants to focus on strategic thinking and creative problem-solving. [14]

AI will enable consultants to offer more personalized and innovative solutions to clients. AI-driven tools will help in developing customized strategies that address specific client needs, improving overall client satisfaction and outcomes.

AI will automate routine and repetitive tasks, freeing up consultants to focus on high-value activities. This will lead to increased efficiency and productivity, allowing consultants to handle more complex and impactful projects. Consultants will leverage AI to experiment with new ideas, optimize business processes, and drive transformational change within organizations. I use AI daily, seeing it as an assistant that is there 24/7, regardless of what time zone I am operating in. It is the crane that can do the heavy lifting. When an email arrives from a prospective client inviting me to speak at his conference, I immediately turn to AI for information about the firm sponsoring the event and its potential audience. Here AI is my thinking companion.

Upon completing a letter of intent to work together with a client, I will have **ChatGPT** review the document and offer a first edit. As history plays an important role in many of the media projects we work with, I get historical information about a title via AI. Sometimes I turn to AI to read about previous transformations that my current project has undergone. Here AI is my research assistant.

PROMPT ENGINEERING: THE MOST IMPORTANT AI SKILL.
No matter which field the consultant is working within, the ability to communicate well with bots is key. The art and science of engineering prompts will be game changing for the consultant who can integrate AI successfully into his projects.

Prompt engineering involves designing and refining input prompts to guide AI models, such as GPT-4, to generate desired outputs. This skill is essential for leveraging AI effectively in various consulting tasks, from data analysis and report generation to strategic planning and client communication. It's said "garbage in, garbage out" when it comes to what we feed the bots. The more detailed and robust the prompt, the better the results. Here are some tips for effective prompt engineering:

 • Craft prompts that are clear, specific, and contextually appropriate. Consultants need to develop the ability to ask precise questions and provide sufficient context to the AI model to elicit useful responses. Don't ask, "What are the latest trends in digital marketing?" Instead, be specific, like the following: "List the top three emerging trends in digital marketing for 2024, with a focus on social media platforms and content types."

 • Provide context and background information to help the AI understand the context better. If you need insights on a market analysis, start with "Considering the recent increase in e-commerce activity due to the pandemic, what are the key factors driving consumer behavior in online shopping?"

 • Structure your prompts with bullet points or numbered lists to make them more organized and easier for the AI to parse. Example: "For a comprehensive report on our client's brand performance, please provide the following details:
  • A summary of recent customer feedback
  • Key performance metrics from the last quarter
  • Recommendations for improving customer satisfaction"

 • Prompt engineering is an iterative process. Consultants should be skilled in refining prompts based on the feedback and results obtained from the AI model. This involves analyzing the AI's output, identifying areas for improvement, and adjusting the prompts accordingly. Sometimes it takes three or more prompts before you and the bot start communicating effectively. Words do the trick when it comes to engineering prompts. Keep changing and adding words until you hit the desired information.

• Indicate how you want the information to be presented, whether as a list, a summary, or a detailed explanation. Example: "Summarize the competitive landscape for the tech industry, focusing on market share, key players, and recent mergers and acquisitions. Provide this information in a bullet-point format."

• Continuously refine your prompts based on the outputs you receive. If the response isn't quite what you need, adjust the prompt to be more precise or include additional details. For example, let's say the initial prompt reads, "What are the challenges in the current media landscape?" and yields a broad response. You can then refine it to "What are the top three challenges faced by digital news outlets in maintaining audience engagement today?"

PROJECT TRACKING.
In 2012, I was doing project tracking to see where we were working and which projects we were still pitching. On projects: Malaysia, Mexico, Norway, USA, UAE, Netherlands, Hong Kong, and Sweden. Pitching: South Africa, USA, Venezuela. The consultant must constantly evaluate the issue of time management. This is different for each individual consultant. Not all projects are going through the same phase. I always imagine that I have a stove with four burners: one on high, one on medium, one on low, and one on simmer. Each day I decide which project goes on what burner. Works for me. Sometimes on busy days, two projects are on high!

In my book **AI: The Next Revolution for Content Creation**, I use the imagery of the dance between humans and robots. Imagine a dance floor where humans and AI partners move together, each contributing their unique strengths and abilities to create a harmonious performance.

The dance between AI and humans is a complex interplay of collaboration, innovation, and shared learning. Humans, with their creativity, intuition, and emotional intelligence, bring a depth of understanding and subjective interpretation to the dance. The bots, with their immense learning of data, bring efficiency, accuracy, and quality control—not to mention speed of delivery. They create a synergy that enhances decision-making.

This is echoed by a study titled *The Crowdless Future? How Generative AI Is Shaping the Future of Human Crowdsourcing* that investigated the capability of generative AI in creating innovative business solutions compared to human crowdsourcing methods: "Results showed comparable quality between human and AI-generated solutions.

"However, human ideas were perceived as more novel, whereas AI solutions delivered better environmental and financial value. We use NLP techniques on the rich solution text to show that although human solvers and GPT-4 cover a similar range of industries of application, human solutions exhibit greater semantic diversity.

"The connection between semantic diversity and novelty is stronger in human solutions, suggesting differences in how novelty is created by humans and AI or detected by human evaluators. This study illuminates the potential and limitations of both human and AI crowdsourcing to solve complex organizational problems and sets the groundwork for a possible integrative human-AI approach to problem-solving." (15)

TOOLS OF THE TRADE
AI as a Multifaceted Consultant

AI can perform various roles similar to a consultant, such as writing, analyzing, coding, and chatting, thereby increasing productivity by handling mundane tasks. Leveraging AI for repetitive and time-consuming activities allows consultants to focus on more strategic and creative aspects of their work. Despite AI's capabilities, human oversight remains crucial to ensure accuracy and relevancy in AI outputs. Combining AI's efficiency with human judgment ensures high-quality outcomes and mitigates AI's limitations, such as errors or hallucinations. AI's ability to analyze cultural contexts and historical influences can help consultants bridge cultural gaps and tailor their strategies to meet client expectations effectively. By integrating AI into the creative workflow, consultants can leverage data-driven insights to develop innovative solutions and stay ahead in their field. Embracing this collaborative dynamic allows consultants to harness AI's capabilities while maintaining the human touch that is essential for empathy, intuition, and moral judgment in consulting.

Passion

Part 4

Passion and Heart

L et's face the facts: There is no quantitative way of measuring passion. But I know when I feel it (most of the time), and I also notice when it is not there, especially for the people around me. There is such a thing as a passion radar, and mine is always on. I can't tell you what my passion radar looks like or where it came from, but passion has little to do with whether a person is introverted or extroverted. Many times, I've seen when the quietest member of the in-house project team is the one with the most passion for the craft.

Passion is not just an emotion; it is a vital component of successful consulting. Passion must drive every aspect of your work, from the initial client meeting to the final execution of ideas. As a consultant, letting your passion shine through in your engagements, designs, and implementations will not only set you apart but also ensure that your work is impactful and transformative. Embrace your passion, and watch as it propels you and your clients toward unprecedented success. Passion has been the driving force behind my every endeavor, whether I'm running a marathon, pursuing a PhD, teaching a grandson about the importance of keeping a diary, or, most importantly, consulting.

It is the engine that fuels my efforts, propelling me to not only meet but exceed expectations. When people ask me when I am planning to retire, my answer is always: "When my passion runs out, when I wake up one morning not feeling the passion to put my shoes on and tackle the task at hand with enthusiasm." The consultant also welcomes passion when spotted within the in-house team. Theater actors are often reminded to spot that one person seated in the front row who seems to be totally engaged with the performance and play.

In advertising, the best copy writing is written from one person to another individual, not for the masses. I've often thought the same applies to our work as consultants. Spot that person in the in-house team who is totally "in" with the project, and make her an ally. The consultant's passion blends with that of the in-house person. Often the most passionate person in the team is not the one with the highest position or seniority, but that does not matter. Each element, from color choice to typeface, should serve these pillars to build a brand that is not only attractive but also strategically sound.

◎ TAKE AIM
Share Your Passion

People often ask me when I plan to retire. My answer is always the same: the day I wake up without the passion to drive innovation, inspire discovery, or witness that pivotal moment when a team fully embraces an idea as their own. That moment when you don't just interpret a project leader's vision but elevate it is what keeps me going. After experiencing more than 700 of these moments throughout my career, I still look forward to the next. If I can ignite that same passion in a team, then I know I've had a truly fulfilling day as a consultant.

The Power of Passion in Consulting

Of all the qualities that contribute to a consultant's success, passion is the most potent and transformative. Passion is the engine that's fueled every one of my endeavors, whether running a marathon, pursuing a PhD, decorating a room, or, most importantly, consulting. It is the engine that fuels my efforts, propelling me to not only meet but exceed expectations. Offering best practices to make passion an integral part of the consultant's work, this chapter will explore the vital importance of passion for a consultant and how it manifests from the very first interaction to the execution of key ideas.

THE FIRST DAY: SETTING THE TONE WITH PASSION.
From the moment you step into a room full of new clients, your passion sets the tone. Your genuine enthusiasm about the project creates an immediate connection. Clients can sense when a consultant is truly invested, and this initial impression lays the groundwork for a successful partnership. Be at your passionate and enthusiastic best!

Passion communicates itself to the client when you keep eye contact with everyone in the room as you speak, when you smile as you present your ideas, and through how you exchange views with everyone present. Listen intently and make comments, sometimes drawing on your own personal experiences. I have found it of interest to relate stories about my early days as a journalism intern with **The Miami News**, in the Miami of the late 1960s, still unsure if I was using the right word in the English language I had just learned.

When I relate these stories, I can see that everyone in the room is paying close attention. When I say, "I am the American dream," the passion of my personal story shines through. I can then continue with my actual presentation, such as "five tips for better mobile storytelling." Passion is personal. Passion is deep-rooted in who you are. I have yet to experience an audience not seduced by the passion I brought to the room.

The element of passion separates one consultant from another. It is not as if you repeat the same stories that reflect your passion at every presentation. Your passion, if you have it, is a huge reservoir of strength, anecdotes, feelings—all at the ready for you to tap into at the right moment.

HOW DO YOU MANIFEST YOUR PASSION?

People often ask me, "How do you manifest your passion?" For me, it's in the energy I make sure I bring into the room, the personal stories I share, and the optimistic belief that transformation is always possible —at any age, under any circumstance. I am usually the oldest person in every room I inhabit as a consultant. Passion isn't just felt; it's seen, heard, and, ultimately, trusted. Here are a few ways I demonstrate my passion while consulting:

· **Energetic engagement:** When you speak to a group for the first time, your energy is palpable. You're not just presenting ideas; you're sharing a vision. Your passion is contagious, inspiring clients to believe in the potential of the project and your ability to lead them toward success. I present my ideas about transformation, then say: "If I can do it, transform myself to accept the way we tell stories in a mobile era, at the age of seventy-seven, so can you." I see smiles in the audience–smiles that translate into action when it comes time to execute my ideas in real time.

• **Authentic communication:** Passionate consultants communicate authentically and with conviction. Your words resonate because they are backed by a deep belief in the work you are doing–as well as your trajectory. It is not just smiling and looking like you are enjoying yourself in front of a room as you speak; it is about dealing with specific case studies. I thought all was lost after I completed ten prototypes and the client rejected them all, but something stronger told me not to give up. I tried one more time, and that was the one version that was accepted, and the project advanced to success. This authenticity fosters trust and respect from clients, which is crucial for effective collaboration.

THE CREATIVE PROCESS: DESIGNING WITH PASSION.
When you sit down to sketch the first designs, passion is your guiding force. This is where your creativity truly shines, and it's evident in every line and concept you develop. If you are passionate, you begin each project as if it were your first. Passion and a blank page (or blank screen) go well together. Passion doesn't clock out once the presentation ends–it fuels the entire journey. I've learned that if you stay committed and energized, your passion becomes the engine that inspires everyone around you to rise to the occasion.
  • **Innovative thinking:** Passion drives you to think outside the box and push your creative boundaries. You're not satisfied with just any solution; you strive for the best possible outcome. This innovative approach ensures that your designs are not only functional but also exceptional. What is the best possible concept for this particular project? I always ask myself that in the early stages of creation. Passion drives me in the creative process and also when I present an idea. Of course, it is passion that helps you when there is rejection on the menu, as if passion taps you on the shoulder and tells you: "Give it another try. You can do it. Go for it."

· **Attention to detail:** A passionate consultant pays meticulous to the details. Every aspect of your design is carefully considered and refined, reflecting your commitment to excellence. This dedication is visible to clients and reinforces their confidence in your expertise. In my experience, passion has led me to be the best that I can be.

EXECUTING IDEAS: PASSION IN ACTION.

Passion doesn't wane after the initial stages; it remains a constant throughout the execution phase. Implementing your ideas with the same fervor ensures that the final product is a true reflection of your vision. You can't fake passion. It's the force that keeps you showing up, pushing forward, and caring deeply at every step of the project–even when the going gets tough. Here are some traits that define the kind of consultant who leads with passion:

· **Relentless pursuit of excellence:** Passionate consultants are dedicated to seeing their ideas through to fruition, overcoming any obstacles that arise. This determination ensures that the end result is of the highest quality.

· **Inspirational leadership:** Your passion inspires and motivates those around you. Whether it's your team or the client's, your enthusiasm encourages everyone to put forth their best effort. This collaborative spirit is essential for achieving outstanding results. I think it is difficult for members of a project team to act apathetic and disinterested when the consultant is full of passion: "If I am passionate about your project, how can you not be?"

FIVE TRAITS OF A PASSION-DRIVEN CONSULTANT.

❝ *Passion guides your first ideas and pushes you to think creatively. It keeps you going through setbacks, and motivates everyone around you to do their best."*

Passion is not just a trait; it is the lifeblood of effective consulting. Those who feel it are lucky, as you can't order it from **Amazon.** Here are the defining traits of a passion-driven consultant:

• **Resilience:** Passionate consultants are resilient in the face of challenges. They view obstacles as opportunities to innovate and improve rather than as setbacks. Remember: Give it another try. You can do it. Go for it.

• **Commitment:** A deep commitment to the project and the client's success is evident. Passionate consultants go above and beyond to ensure that their work delivers value.

• **Empathy:** Passion drives a strong sense of empathy, enabling consultants to understand and address client needs effectively. This empathetic approach fosters strong, lasting relationships. Your passion may be contagious. I have received correspondence from clients several years after the completion of a project with messages like: "I will always remember the passion that you brought to our newsroom. It is still there, and we quote you often."

• **Curiosity:** A passionate consultant is always curious, eager to learn and explore new ideas and methodologies. This curiosity leads to continuous improvement and staying ahead of industry trends. A passionate consultant makes sure that a sense of childlike curiosity prevails during the entire project.

• **Integrity:** Passionate consultants operate with a high level of integrity. They are honest, transparent, and dedicated to doing what is right for the client and the project. And they are not afraid to keep trying until they get it right. Passion pushes you to advance to the finish line.

AI-ASSISTED PASSION AND CREATIVITY.

There is much discussion today about the creative wonders of AI. Consider Botnik, an AI program that can write its own **Harry Potter** chapters, [1] or **DALL-E** and **Midjourney**, which create images with specified visual styles based on text input.

Here is where human passion comes into play: While the majority of current AI-creativity research aims to develop tools that may replace human input rather than support human creative performance, I believe that the ideal framework is, again, the dance between human and robot, a framework making suggestions for AI support instead of replacement. It is the collaboration between the human with passion and ideas and the robot helping to carry out those ideas. A study about AI-assisted creativity summarized it best: "AI-generated stimulus ideas can be used to inspire human creativity and reduce cognitive fixation on innovation platforms. Thereby, AI can either generate novel ideas or customize the presentation of user-generated ideas on innovation platforms (e.g., showing highly dissimilar versus very similar ideas)." [2]

THE PASSION OF DALÍ.

When I think of passion, the great artist Salvador Dalí comes to mind. Whether you like his style—the melting clocks, repeated use of roses or crutches or dragons in his art—Dalí's surrealistic approach is characterized by intense passion and boundless creativity. When viewing Dalí's paintings, I see an artist's unbound passion with everything on the canvas.

Similarly, when you, as a consultant, are in front of a project group, everyone there should perceive that you are not just an expert on the subject but that you are passionate about it. Passion inspires. Passion sells ideas. The passion with which you present your ideas is a sure way to catapult your project to a highly successful completion.

THREE FEELINGS PREVAIL IN THAT FIRST TIME MEETING, 2010.
On April 8, 2010, I wrote these three words in my diary: anxiety, ignorance, and excitement. Those are the prevailing feelings when a project team meets the consultant: anxiety of wondering how each member will fare with the demands of the project and the consultant; ignorance and the feeling that one does not know enough about the subject to be a good contributing participant; and excitement, the promise of what's to come.

When the project succeeds, you know you were part of something big that brought positive results to the company. You will be noticed. Promoted. You become part of the company's history.

BE PATIENT WITH THE CEO WHO IS NOT "WITH IT."
In 2010, I was sitting in a conference room listening to a CEO as he introduced me to a project that involved transformation to digital. Yet I heard him say: "Is paper, printed newspapers, really dying? I don't believe so, with all due respect.

"A newspaper experience is unique, allows you to be alone with your paper, no interruptions, no beeps, no phone ringing, all those devices that drive us crazy. How can we strike a balance between connected and disconnected?" I waited my turn for what was supposed to be a ten-minute introduction ("I will be brief") but had turned into an ode to print media, accentuated with historical touches taking us back to 2500 BC. He mentioned Plato, Shakespeare, Thoreau, and Benjamin Franklin.

Following him, I was supposed to talk about all things mobile and digital. All went well, digital was discussed, good questions were asked, and the project succeeded in getting that publication to a digital-first strategy. This instance, documented in my diary, emphasized that, as consultants, once we leave home, we are at the mercy of the elements (not just the weather), the cast of characters in our midst, and the surprises of serendipity.

A KEY QUESTION IN MICHIGAN, USA.
On April 15, 2003, I had my first coffee meeting in the publisher's office in Grand Rapids, Michigan. He asked, "Do we have the people to execute this project?" So here I was, hired to do a major redesign and rethink of this regional newspaper. The contract had been signed.

When the publisher asked that question, I shivered a bit. After all, he must know his people well. What do I know, since I have not met anyone? Ironically, when I later met with the project team, the first question from them was, "How do you effect change?"

Fortunately, as usually happens, he did have the right people, and the project succeeded. I have noticed that many times the CEO of the company may have little regard for the talents of the people working in his organization. It is something that has always surprised me, and you may encounter the same. In most cases, talents exist that a CEO is unaware of. It is the role of the consultant to make sure he knows. Careers can be saved. The CEO here warmed up to the project as soon as the first prototype samples were available. His enthusiasm surged when he found out that advertisers had loved the new design and how their ads gained prominence. Consultants: Beware of the CEOs who play the devil's advocate role sometimes for self-importance but more often to challenge their teams to question what the consultant has to offer.

Sometimes the admired, experienced CEO with the shiny glass desk with a splendid view of the mountains needs more hand-holding and teddy bears than anyone in his team.

WHEN THE CLIENT IS NERVOUS.
I was in Vienna in 2009, headed for a meeting with the editor and project manager. The last four days, I had noticed how this editor was

extremely nervous about our project—more so than what I usually observe. I had to put a plan in action for this morning meeting, where I told him to put his fears aside. "The project will work," I assured him. Then I asked him to reevaluate the work of his newsroom, and I reassured him that his editors would quickly adapt and reminded him of how much readers would like the new product. He was simply one of those clients who needed constant hand-holding. So, remember, sometimes the consultant is also an elementary school teacher.

FINE-TUNING YOUR METHODOLOGY.
Way back on November 11, 1981, I was in Canada, working on a project for **The Edmonton Journal**. I wrote detailed notes after the first meeting with this team, wanting it to be perfect and not leave out any of the observations discussed.

When I looked back at my notes from this project, not only was my handwriting more legible than now, but the outline of my thoughts was detailed and easy to follow. If I needed to, I could have proceeded and created a design concept from the specific notes, even in 2025. As you gain experience, your note-taking will become faster and spottier. Part of developing a methodology includes how you record your thoughts, not just the ones discussed during a meeting, but also bursts of ideas that may happen at any time. Keep those cocktail napkins handy—and, of course, your Notes app on your smartphone, although I still prefer to jot things down on paper whenever possible. As much as I love modern tools, you'll still find my Moleskine notebook by my side at all times. Don't let that possible great idea get away!

SOMETIMES IT'S DIFFICULT TO DRAW ON PASSION.
This lesson came to the forefront with a project in Chile, an unforgettable one because the date we had picked to launch the redesigned newspaper happened to be September 12, 2001. We media consultants always pray that no major news breaks on the day that we unveil the new look of a newspaper or magazine. No such luck here.

This project had been difficult from the start.

What happens when the CEO/managing director exercises such a powerful grip on the organization that many new ideas are immediately discarded? When less than half of what the consultant proposes make it to the project finish line? That's when even the most passionate consultant needs to reach out for an extra protein smoothie.

I have spent an entire career as a sort of change salesman. I arrive, I put change on the table, and I ask for tasters. Some taste with gusto; others want to but are afraid. Of course, the moment they call a consultant, the people in the organization are aware that change is in order; accepting it later is a different story.

At **El Mercurio,** it was no different. We presented one prototype after the other, starting with the most adventurous, daring, and contemporary—which were quickly taken off the walls of that grand library of the newspaper where we were doing the presentations. Next came a modern but not so daring prototype: "Oh... the photos are too big. What happens to our longer texts?" Okay, back to the drawing board.

Finally, we had it: a mere face wash of the existing **El Mercurio.** Nothing much had changed: The lead photo would be small and the text abundant, and so we were ready for launch on September 12, 2001. For context, here is my diary entry from the day:

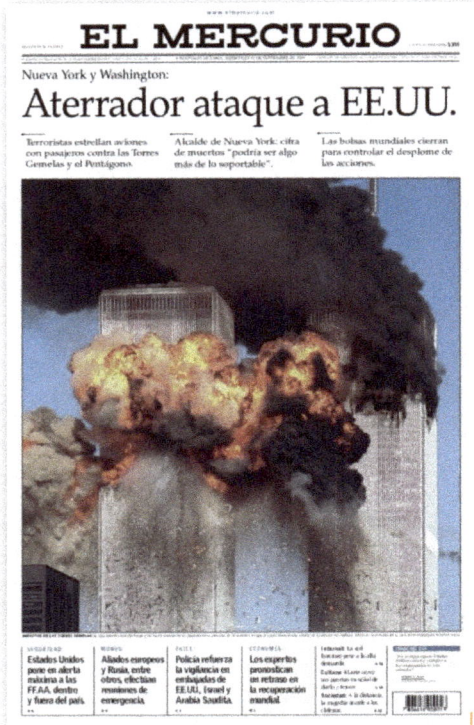

*The morning of September 12, 2001, after I finished my 37-minute run thinking about the perils and nervousness of change, I returned to my room. I turned on **CNN** and proceeded to do my stretching on the floor.*

Suddenly, the woman anchor said something about breaking news: "A plane has hit one of the

*Twin Towers in New York City." That was that. Was it a small plane?
"No further details yet," she said. Developing story. I emerged from
the shower a few minutes later to become aware of the full horror of
the story. Then I knew that once we got to the newsroom, we had to
get into WHAT IF mode of the kind nobody had prepared us for. This
was not an anticipated death of someone famous or infamous. These
were, indeed, the what -if pages of all pages. I knew that it would not
be a small photo on page one of the first day of the "new"* **El Mercurio**
after all.

I remember sitting in front of the computer, looking at photos to
pick for the front page, tears running down my cheeks. I was the only
American in the room, and it all hurt badly. Change ruled the day.

Change ruled the next few days. Change ruled the decade. Change
that still haunts us in many of the things we do every day. So I was
thinking, of change: Why is change so difficult to accept? Sometimes
as a consultant it's important to remember that there are powerful
outside forces that also affect the audience's and the client's passion—a
different sort of passion that has to be accounted for.

PASSION LEADS TO REINVENTION.
*"Striving for knowledge is the essential, golden rule. In consulting,
you can't survive without having deep understanding and knowledge.
It can be knowledge about the industry you're working in, or about
your specific project or full comprehension of the frameworks one
uses and relies on." —Dr. Sandeep K. Krishnan* (3)

As a consultant who conducts himself with passion and a sense of
responsibility for the advice he offers clients, it is imperative to be constantly reinventing. Continue to update your knowledge.

Subscribe to newsletters in your field so that you have daily access
to the most current information. There's rarely a morning I don't find
two or three stories of interest in my daily readings that help me update
my next presentation. Updated information is the best capital you have
to offer your clients. With knowledge comes constant renovations and

reinventions. Knowledge gives you confidence, a key element to establish authority and credibility with the client.

Reinvention should be organic. The business landscape is constantly evolving–especially in my own field of media consulting. I always say that I have lived through six revolutions since the start of my own career, in 1969, with the last two of those revolutions being the switch to mobile content creation and the arrival of AI. Both have been highly pivotal moments for newsrooms around the world. As a consultant, I would be less effective without diving into these two areas to learn as much as possible about them. As a result, my work as a consultant carries more weight.

HOW DOES ONE TACKLE REINVENTION?
The people I work with in the media do have a passion for what they do. Specifically for journalists, passion surges when there is a breaking story of consequence. Imagine September 11, the ultimate breaking news with major consequence, and I had a front row seat with the team of **El Mercurio,** seeing those journalists, photographers, and illustrators oblivious to the clock, marching forward to provide the best coverage of that monumental story for the readers.

A strong sense of curiosity gets you to the door of reinvention: In my industry, more people are reading news and consuming information on a mobile device. So, we ask ourselves, How does this change the way we create content? Indeed, the way we consume news on mobile devices changes how we write, edit, and design. After doing a ton of research, which included getting onto the New York Metro Subway and passing from car to car observing how people consumed news on their phones, I was able to start experimenting with various styles of mobile storytelling, leading to the publication of my trilogy, **The Story,** devoted to Transformation-Storytelling-Design for a mobile-first world. My own curiosity led me there.

This curiosity must extend beyond surface-level observations. In any industry, consultants should immerse themselves in the environment of their clients, analyzing trends, consumer behaviors, and technological disruptions. Whether you're advising a retail company navigating the shift to e-commerce, a health-care provider embracing telemedicine, or a logistics firm integrating AI-driven automation, curiosity opens the door to discovery. It also makes the job more fun.

As AI kicked the door open in every field, I took note, making mental notes that then translated into action: Get **ChatGPT,** start communicating with the bots, attend seminars about AI, get your hands on books about it. Indeed, I am often told that I am the oldest person in the world discussing AI. This is not about age, though.

This is about having a child's curiosity at any age and the passion to face the new, even when you are chronologically old.

One does not last as a consultant without constant reinvention. The clients expect it. Reinventing yourself is one of the most pleasant experiences. It gives you vigor and hope and keeps you young.

Reinventing is part of what makes continuous learning fun. In the process, you, the consultant, adopt new technologies and integrate new tools into your work processes, which clients benefit from.

When you reinvent yourself, you engage in experimentation, try out new techniques. Mobile storytelling is quite different from the way stories are crafted for a print publication, for example. For print, text is never interrupted with images. One sees photos, then reads the stories. It is the opposite with mobile, where the text narrative is woven with visual assets.

In the process of reinventing yourself, you develop a new network of contacts, leading to new relationships and consulting opportunities.

GREAT IDEA
Show Your Passion

Passion is a vital component that drives every aspect of a consultant's work, from initial client meetings to final executions. Embracing and showcasing passion can propel both the consultant and the client toward unprecedented success, ensuring that the work is impactful and transformative. Passion sets the tone from the first interaction, creating an immediate connection. Passion is the guiding force in the creative process, driving innovative thinking and meticulous attention to detail. Passionate consultants strive for exceptional outcomes, pushing creative boundaries and ensuring that every detail is refined and considered. Passionate consultants overcome obstacles and maintain high quality standards, inspiring collaboration and achieving outstanding results. Passionate consultants dedicate themselves to their clients' success; continuously improve; and maintain strong, lasting relationships based on trust and empathy.

ANTICIPATING TOMORROW.
"You don't grow in the consulting profession by getting better at what you've already done yesterday. You grow by anticipating tomorrow."
—Alan Weiss

Call it the consultant's antenna, or the dog's nose. Or a result of the passion you feel for your field. In any case, an alert consultant is not only keeping up with the trends affecting his field in the present but also anticipating the topics that may change the craft in the future.

As you see, I became an author, and I attribute my success as a consultant to my books, which reached into every corner of the world, leading to invitations for me to "come help us with our newspaper." While "publish or perish" has traditionally been a mandate for academics, I would dare say it should be the same for consultants who wish to get their message across before they pay a first visit to a prospective client.

In the late 1970s, as a young professor at Syracuse University's Newhouse School of Public Communications, I observed that editors were becoming more conscious of how their newspapers looked. The term "newspaper makeup" was replaced by "newspaper design." Layout editors were now art directors. It was time to get some guidelines for how to design newspapers. I wrote **Contemporary Newspaper Design: A Structural Approach**, which had three different editions and served as my springboard to the world of national and international consulting.

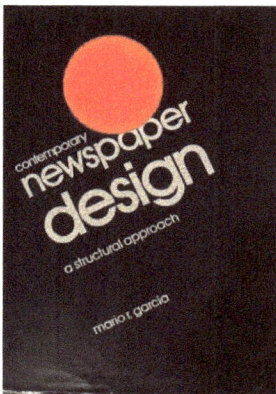

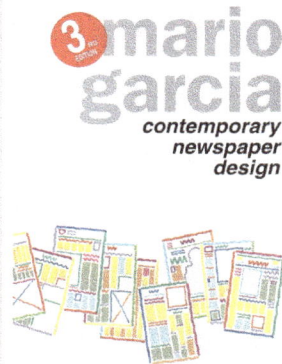

In the late 1980s, I knew that newspapers were on their way to a transformation from printing in black and white to introducing color because many newspaper nameplates (logos) were in color. While not many newspapers had color printing machines, they could do the so-called spot color—a line in color, or the background color in a box. Better things were to come. I seized the opportunity to learn more about color. But, of course, there was no **Google** or **ChatGPT** to go to and retrieve an instant encyclopedic treatment on the subject. I realized that the one other industry that had made the transformation from black and white to color was the movies. Flying to Los Angeles, I met with some old-timers who had been involved in the process and learned much about color perception and how the eye moves on a horizontal screen (similar to a horizontal newspaper page) and came back fully charged from Hollywood.

The Poynter EyeTrack Studies

In the 1980s, I became fascinated by how readers actually read—not just what they said they liked but where their eyes really went on the page. That curiosity led me and my Poynter Institute colleague Dr. Pegie Stark to conduct some of the first eye-track studies in journalism, and those findings became the foundation for my early books on visual storytelling and news design. I find myself quoting the reports of those EyeTrack tests to audiences that were not even born yet when the studies were conducted.

- **Eyes on the News (1991):** Directed by Dr. García and Dr. Pegie Stark, this pioneering study examined reader interactions with print newspapers, focusing on elements like color and photography.

- **EyeTrack07 (2007):** As an advisor, Dr. García contributed to this study comparing reading behaviors across broadsheet, tabloid, and online formats.

- **EyeTrack: Tablet (2012):** Dr. García collaborated with Poynter to investigate how users read news on tablets, providing insights into tablet navigation and user engagement.

Suddenly, I was a "newspaper color expert." Yes, just like that. I have learned that you become an expert when your curiosity drags you passionately in a certain direction. In 1986, I wrote **Color in American Newspapers,** followed in 1988 by the more global **Newspaper Colour Design,** which appeared in four languages simultaneously. Now I was a certified color expert, the consultant so many newspapers called when they wanted to colorize their pages. I transformed about 200 newspapers from black and white to color, including **The Journal**–the project of projects.

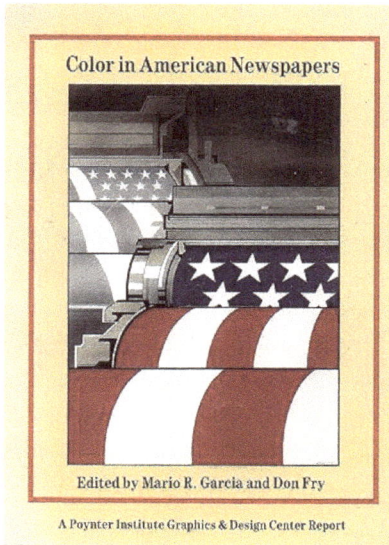

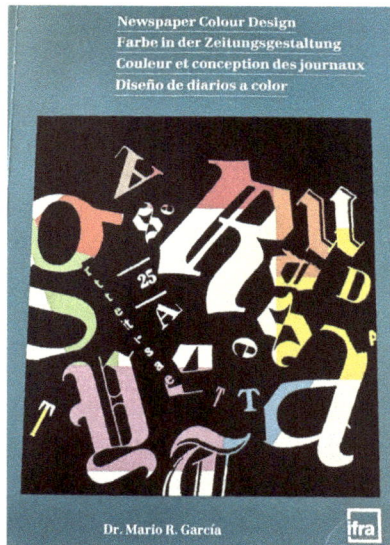

The next big revolution–and demand for change–came with the arrival of the internet, around 1991. Again, editors did not consider how this would be important or consequential. Usually, a newspaper's internet team consisted of a group of youngsters, with the senior editors barely paying attention to what they did as they "played in their sandbox."

But that sandbox was becoming more important with each day, and the editors' refusal to give it proper attention has had effects on the industry that we still feel today. I immediately observed the importance of the internet—and felt driven to write my next book, **Redesigning Print for the Web.** The media executives were not the only ones to ignore and resist the internet. The internet's arrival disrupted established business practices on a global scale, reshaping the foundations of commerce and industry. It was timely to be present to tackle this issue.

The pattern of dismissal of the internet was profoundly deep, extending across industries. For example, in retail, giants like Sears and JCPenney dismissed e-commerce as a passing fad, while new-comers like **Amazon** quietly built their empires. Established retailers viewed online shopping as a supplemental, niche channel rather than a primary one, ignoring how quickly consumer behavior was evolving. In entertainment, the music industry initially resisted digital distribution and the rise of MP3s. Even in the travel industry, airlines and travel agencies failed to fully anticipate how the internet would empower consumers. In the same manner, when **Apple** introduced the iPad, on April 3, 2010, global newspaper executives saw it as the next platform where news would be consumed.

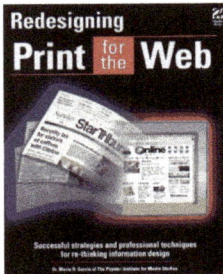

Newsrooms everywhere were abuzz with the excitement of producing tablet editions. Major publications like **The New York Times**, **The Journal,** and **USA Today** launched dedicated iPad apps almost immediately. This was going to be the next big wave of how consumers reached the news. There were a couple new factors when it came to reading news on iPads:

• **Enhanced interactivity:** Publishers experimented with interactive content, multimedia integration, and dynamic layouts to leverage the iPad's touch interface.

• **Subscriptions and paywalls:** The iPad's ecosystem facilitated new business models, including in-app subscriptions and paywalls, providing a new revenue stream for struggling print media.

Looking back, the dreams many publishers had for the iPad did not come to materialize. According to a Statista 2024 survey, 60 percent

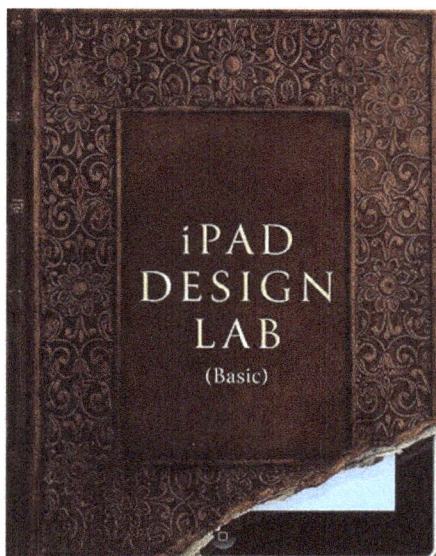

iPAD
DESIGN
LAB
(Basic)

of US respondents owned an iPad, making it the leading tablet brand in the country.

About 34 percent of adults report reading news on a tablet at least once a week. (4)

Older readers love their tablets, and the majority of those reading news on tablets are between fifty and older, with the sixty-five-plus age group dominating this market.

Tablet news consumption is higher in Europe than in the US. (5) While the iPad may not have completely revolutionized the media landscape as some early proponents expected, it has significantly influenced the way digital content is consumed and has driven innovation in the publishing industry. Industry predictions do not always come true.

Its role in the shift toward mobile-first content consumption cannot be understated. As I conducted workshops, I was getting more requests for training on writing and designing specifically for the tablet.

The result? My book **The iPad Lab: Storytelling in the Age of the Tablet** appeared in 2011, and the demand for my consulting services and workshops related to the tablet kept me busy around the world. I centered my consulting around two major themes related to the iPad:

• **Changing habits:** My workshops and presentations covered how the iPad changed reading habits and the consumption of news, with readers increasingly expecting rich, multimedia content.

• **Business models:** I discussed new business models enabled by the iPad, such as digital subscriptions and in-app purchases, and their implications for the future of journalism, highlighting how these innovations could enhance content accessibility and diversify revenue streams for publishers.

The Story

BY MARIO GARCIA

TRANSFORMATION, STORYTELLING, AND DESIGN IN THE MOBILE NEWS MOVEMENT

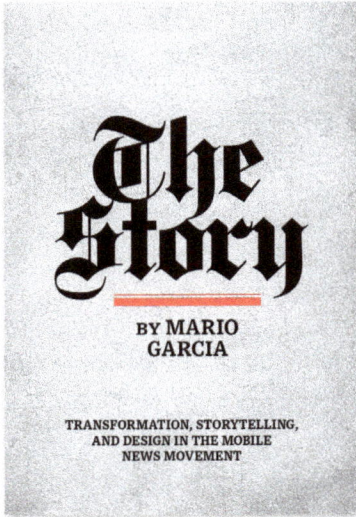

As more readers started reading on their phones and other mobile devices, the time was right to research how to write/edit/design for mobile.

Mobile storytelling was at the top of my consulting menu, and dozens of newsroom executives—today, close to one hundred—demanded my services to conduct mobile storytelling workshops for their teams.

After conducting several of these workshops, my book **The Story** (6) appeared as a trilogy: Transformation/Storytelling/Design.

Tablets have revolutionized many other industries by offering a streamlined, user-friendly interface and mobility that aligns with how people operate in today's tech-savvy world. Think of that tablet you were handed at the doctor's office to fill out a form or the one in the hand of the waiter at the restaurant for taking orders. Also, brands like **Apple, Sephora,** and **Best Buy** use tablets as portable point-of-sale systems, inventory checkers, and product information tools.

AI has come knocking on the doors of every business globally as an unstoppable tsunami. For journalists, it is a helpful tool to save time on basic research. The consultant must be tuned in to those developments that impact his craft, staying ahead of technological shifts to deliver cutting-edge solutions. Aware of the impact of AI, I began to research it, dipping my toes into the world of AI—via **ChatGPT.** The fascination with AI was instant. That's how I started writing **AI: The Next Revolution in Content Creation** (7) and, of course, how AI became part of my consultant's palette of offerings. Today, half of my work is about AI and content creation.

Curiosity and a passion for learning new things found me spending about forty-five minutes daily sharing coffee and time with the robot that I imagined sitting next to me—sometimes at the window seat during a flight, on my sofa at home in New York, and, I must confess,

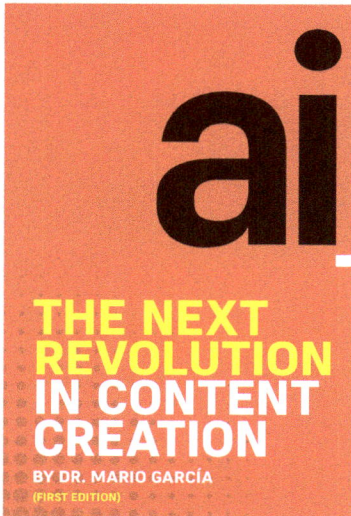

THE NEXT
REVOLUTION
IN CONTENT
CREATION
BY DR. MARIO GARCÍA
(FIRST EDITION)

under my beach umbrella in Florida. Curiosity and passion are the twin engines that drive lifelong learning and reinvention. These qualities not only fuel personal growth but also enable us to adapt to an ever-changing world. This is required for the consultant who wishes to stay in demand.

In essence, the commitment to continual learning and reinvention is not just a professional necessity that can benefit you as a professional consultant but also a deeply personal journey that expands our horizons.

I often remind myself of how important a curious mind is to make the job of the consultant more fun and efficient.

TAKE AIM
Anticipating the Next Trend Helps the Consultant

The successful consultant emphasizes the importance of foresight, adaptability, and continual learning in the consulting profession. Pay attention to technological advancements. Be curious and passionate, which are key to continuous learning and professional reinvention. By continually updating your knowledge and skills, you will remain a valuable resource for clients navigating these changes. By staying ahead of industry trends and continually expanding your expertise, you maintain a dynamic and influential presence in the consulting world—which leads to steady work.

You've Gotta Have Heart

I was invited to participate at a Society for News Design conference in Cleveland. In a closing ceremony game, three of us panelists were on stage and had two minutes to explain what we considered to be a "pivotal story." It was up to us to choose our own story. The audience, of course, was made up of designers, editors, and students.

I thought a lot about what a pivotal story would be for me. After forty years as a professional, I already knew then that I could not come up with just one story. There have been many pivotal stories in my life, as readers of my blog and of the "40 Years/40 Lessons" series know well.

How can one select a single story when you have been a child actor, a teenage refugee, a husband, a father, a grandfather, a designer, a professor, a consultant, and an author? It has been a rich and interesting life, with exhilarating moments of personal triumph, and low and sad moments, like the loss of my wife and my mother.

But when I had to choose what I consider to be a pivotal moment, I knew that it had something to do with the heart. You've got to have heart. It may sound cliché to say that you've got to have heart, but you do.

And having heart does not make you "better" or holier than thou. Not at all. Life is easier when you have a heart because it is the heart that allows us to put ourselves, even momentarily, in the shoes of the people we are interacting with. Of course, it is the brain that guides us through so many of the processes involved in our daily lives, and especially our work. But the brain is only part of the equation.

The heart is the brain's ideal sidekick. It is the heart that flashes a yellow light between the green and the red. It is the heart that may keep us from saying something we may regret moments later. It is the heart that may cut through what may be instant anger to buffer that feeling while you try to understand what made you so angry. Ironically, the very project that once provoked anger can unexpectedly transform into a source of pure joy, filling your heart with a moment of total bliss.

For me, this was in Germany with **Die Zeit,** referenced here and elsewhere as the most difficult project of my career. Yet, when completed, it was the most well received and award winning. My heart accelerated with joy every time **Die Zeit** was chosen Best-Designed Newspaper in the World1 and to see the pride and satisfaction of the team as they received all those bravo accolades. **Die Zeit** is a powerhouse dynasty in the news media world—akin to the New York Yankees in their legacy and dominance in Major League Baseball. For over forty years, since this global distinction has been awarded, they have consistently ranked among the most successful news organizations.

I worked with **Die Zeit** off and on for about three years. Perhaps most notably, when Dieter von Holtzbrinck bought the title, it was archaic—there were no photos, no art directors. I was the chief architect of its first transformation into what later became a sophisticated brand driven by a stable of very talented art directors.

They deserve the credit for the weekly visual surprises that make their publication so great. It's a welcome reminder that the consultant breaks the ice, tears down the walls to allow for more openness, and hammers hard on the foundations that then lead to a product that the in-house team can nourish and make thrive for the long term.

THE HEART AS COPILOT.

In specific terms, having a heart has helped me through many instances when a difficult student in one of my classes refused to play by the rules. Or when an art director in one of my projects can't get over the fact that he now has a consultant to deal with and feels that his bosses do not trust him and/or his talents to carry out the project. The heart also helps when dealing with everyday situations, rude service providers, less-than-cordial colleagues, and the ever-present pessimists who always find the hole in the donut.

I don't know how you can "get a heart" if you don't already have one. I assume it is there for us to tap into it. Throughout my long career, I have allowed my brain to be the captain in the cockpit, with the heart as an alert copilot.

I get angry just like everyone else, but not easily. When it does happen, my first reaction is to wonder if the anger is justified. *Pick your battles, Mario*, my brain reminds me. *Is it possible that you made someone angry, Mario?* asks my heart. Like everyone else, I run into all the emotions and reactions of the human condition. Remember that I spend most of my time in newsrooms, interacting with creative people. Some of them are quite smart and talented but can also be heartless.

I have witnessed the very talented with no patience for the less so, the one in a high position stepping over those under his supervision, the person in power surrounding himself with his favorites at the expense of the real talent who is not part of the clique. These are the exceptions. In the majority of cases, I have seen the brainy and talented with the biggest hearts: the ones who are so self-assured that they surround themselves with the best, and everyone shines (guided by the heart).

Life is definitely easier, our interactions more pleasant, and the result of our work more successful and everlasting if we let the heart guide us in those moments that defy logic. Some of the most successful people I have ever worked with and the best professors and bosses I have had the honor of encountering have had heart. The heart keeps us going in more ways than one.

The best managers I have worked with are firm, fair, and compassionate. Those are the three characteristics of people for whom the heart is, indeed, the pivotal story. It is no different for consultants.

Navigating the sometimes rough waters of a consulting engagement is always easier if the consultant has a heart. Let's talk about the heart figuratively. While you probably have your heart, the organ, checked regularly via doctor's visits, nurturing your heart—the soulful one—requires that you develop your own rituals and activities. I have a friend who does consulting on color, and she uses meditation and yoga to nourish her soulful heart. Personally, I have done a morning run through many cities around the world at the start of the day to help me process the consulting challenges. I also find that keeping a diary, even a simple one with a one-sentence entry for the day, is comforting and helps the heart and the mind focus on what's important.

TEDDY BEARS.

As a consultant, I am aware of the importance of teddy bears. They exist, and not just for kids, believe me. I dispense teddy bears to my clients—not real ones, as you will see—but I also sometimes ask my clients to shoot the teddy bears that bind them. Let me explain.

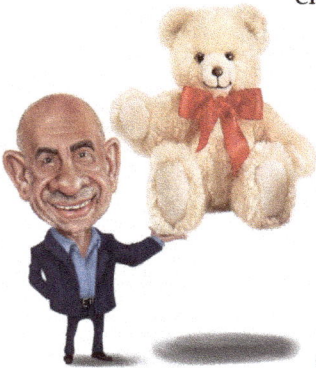

It is not that I have any physical teddy bears with me as I travel globally from project to project. But if I were to literally pass out teddy bears, I would give out more than Santa Claus. Let's discuss the symbolic importance of teddy bears. What is a "teddy bear," in my definition of the term?

Teddy bears offer reassurance. As a consultant, on those first meetings to kick off a project, I pass out teddy bears that are my way of saying, "This is going to be all right at the end." I am the outsider who just landed in this organization, but I must be able to feel the fear and skepticism of the in-house team. They are close to the existing product that we are there to change. They, in many cases, built that product. There are ties, attachments, and even affection for the product as is, even if they are aware that it needs change.

The world needs a lot of teddy bears. We all do. Like the in-house team who is afraid that moving to digital-first may hurt the brand, who does not have a doubt or two, or three?

In today's newsrooms, those doubts are multiplied because we are in an industry in transition. Nobody knows what newspapers will be like in three or five years. So for those involved in the media today, teddy bears are not just important; they are essential. When a publisher is fearful of putting up paywalls to get revenue for content, the teddy bear is a gentle reminder that if there is good content, people are willing to pay for it. When an editor wonders if he will have a job two years from now, the teddy bear is a reminder that, of course, he will have a job, but it may require reinventing, rethinking, and learning new ways.

When an art director feels less than adequate in the presence of the consultant who has been hired to assist him, the teddy bear is a reminder that all is well, that he has the talent but that the consultant has the experience to take the project from here to there.

When a student doubts that she is majoring in the right field, simply because she has received C+ marks in two consecutive projects, the teddy bear is there to remind her that school is a phase for learning, discovering, and improving and should not signal the end of a career dream.

When one of my grandkids wants to learn to play guitar instantly or to master a social studies chapter in fifteen minutes prior to a test, the teddy bear is a reminder that nothing is instant, that it takes perseverance. So, as a consultant, I've often found myself dispensing many teddy bears in the form of delivering encouragement, reassurance, or empathy in some fashion.

Teddy bears make reassurance a leadership tool.

Teddy bears are great teachers, often without saying one word.

Teddy bears soothe.

Teddy bears remind us of the child in everyone.

Teddy bears usually bring a smile to the face of the recipient. I need teddy bears as much as the next guy. We all do throughout life. It is a lucky day for the consultant—and happens sometimes—when the client appears at the door of the next meeting with a teddy bear to offer the consultant. The occasions I'm reminded of often involved the sudden replacement of a project leader who was not holding his own.

"We are replacing John with Mary," the project director will tell me. Bliss. Or "Mario, we are looking into getting the content management system that you recommend for us to excel with mobile storytelling."

However, teddy bears do not have to be big moments like these examples. A teddy bear appears during that first coffee of the morning when the CEO says: "I think your ideas are already beginning to have a good effect here." Sometimes getting your own office space with a view for when you are working in-house or ensuring that you have an ample supply of Pellegrino sparkling water makes a difference. Or, as happened in India, a steady flow of homemade curries especially prepared by the CEO's home chef.

Every industry faces moments of transition, and with those transitions come fears, doubts, and resistance. Whether it's the in-house team at a legacy retailer worried that embracing e-commerce will erode the personal touch of their brand or a manufacturing team uneasy about automation replacing familiar processes, doubt is universal.

For industries undergoing rapid transformation, the need for reassurance and support is magnified. In finance, employees grapple with the implications of AI-driven analytics and blockchain disrupting traditional banking. In health care, practitioners question how telemedicine and wearable technology will redefine patient care.

In education, teachers and administrators worry about the rise of online platforms and the implications for in-person learning. Who doesn't have a question or two—or twenty—when change is on the horizon? Those teddy bears of reassurance have never been more important.

THE OTHER TEDDY BEARS THAT BIND.
We cling to our teddy bears. We clutch them tightly to our hearts—and to our heads. The consultant walks into a room where everyone in the project group is clutching his teddy bear. Those are the teddy bears of myths and legacies. "We could never use that much color here; our audience would reject it." "The only typefaces that would work here would be serifs, and not too bold." "We don't have the talent in the art department to carry out that level of design and illustrations." "Our older readers don't read on digital devices at all."

Those are teddy bears that impede progress and transformation, which is why I sometimes can be heard saying: "Shoot those teddy bears immediately." That was the case in one of my favorite projects, with **American City Business Journals (ACBJ)**, the Charlotte-based publisher of local business news in over forty cities across the US. Our project goal was to retool their weekly print editions for the contemporary media environment. We sought to create a printed product that could "connect the dots" for readers, providing analysis to buttress the news **ACBJ** breaks online 24/7. Here were forty weeklies across the US, all with a different look. The project was referred to internally as "Pinstripe," since my team and I had created a unique branding look for all forty titles using a pinstripe, seen here.

After establishing as a project goal that one model would be created for all forty **ACBJ** markets, we developed multiple prototypes that explored distinct ideas of what a modern local business weekly could be.

I must share with you my experience when we were about to start our first exploratory workshop with the **ACBJ** top management in Charlotte. Folded side by side on a table near the CEO's office were copies of the forty weekly newspapers that we were about to analyze in depth, each with its own distinctive nameplate, typography, look, and feel. Some were quite advanced in their design and overall visual presentation—others not so much. But all were unified by excellent local business journalism, which is what distinguishes the titles and grants them enormous respect from their readers.

Honestly, it is okay for a consultant to have a feeling like that early during a project: I could not imagine unifying all these titles in cities as diverse as San Francisco and Phoenix and Atlanta and Tampa. I believe I said, "This is a chamber of horrors" in terms of design.

"I well remember your 'chamber of horrors' assessment," said Emory Thomas (2), chief content officer for **ACBJ.** "That shortcoming was the reason I contacted you to begin with! The design decisions we then made together paved the way for a profound upgrade of both our publications and our ability to attract design talent."

We opted to concentrate our efforts in that first workshop to imagining and creating the ultimate business weekly for today. We were working with print, of course, but never letting go of how our efforts would affect what is done with digital. I realized I had to imagine creating one modern weekly print newspaper and not think of unifying forty existing ones. We, as consultants, sometimes get blindsided by the magnitude of one aspect of the project instead of cutting the large pizza into slices and going for the slice that is digestible. As I was thinking about the transformation of forty weeklies, I was not spending time thinking about one and applying the changes and lessons learned on that one to the other thirty-nine. It's much easier to start with one aspect of the project, then branch out into applications for the rest. Here is how Emory Thomas, still chief content officer for **American City Business Journals**, remembers that day:

That first meeting was a small group of editors. (It was soon after that that we brought other departments into the discussion.) And I recall well Mario's reaction to the forty-title chore ahead. He literally sank in his chair as he pondered the complexity of the project. I was sure he was about to walk out the door.

But when we turned the conversation back to the core mission, he re-engaged. Yes, we have dozens of independent publications, but they all needed a new model to follow, one that was built from the ground up for a digital age.

We were, after all, re-imagining the operation of a local business newsroom that would produce excellent, made-for-the-medium content for every major platform—web, mobile, print, and tablet. Each of these platforms needed a rethink, in relation to the other, so that we could update and raise our game both online and in print.

This required fully recognizing, and delivering, what readers wanted from each. We focused on print, in part because this was our legacy product, but it's been a multiplatform project from the outset. It was a unique experience in which editors, managers, production, advertising and marketing people sat around the table to shape the new ideas.

That was in 2013 when he wrote that, but Emory Thomas recently recalled the Pinstripe project fondly: *As I look back on the Pinstripe initiative—encompassing a tectonic shift to digital-forward publishing, complete redesign, unification of branding both company-and product-wide, creation of new recruitment narratives for talent, and more—I think of it in three phases, maybe four. Philosophy, architecture, sales, implementation. And then of course there was the follow through policing.*

📎 **SAVE IT**
Always Have a Heart

Having heart in consulting isn't just a cliché—it's a cornerstone of truly effective practice. A consultant with heart can connect deeply, understanding and sharing the perspectives of others. It's not only about talent; it's about striking a balance between expertise and empathy. Heart fosters emotional intelligence, enabling meaningful and authentic engagement. While technical skills are essential, it's heart that ultimately drives lasting impact and genuine relationships in the professional world.

THE CONSULTANT AS TRAVELER.
In the process of traveling for consulting projects, I have also developed a passion for discovering new places; meeting new, interesting people; and learning from all those little experiences that contribute to making our journey more fascinating and enriching.

The world is my neighborhood.

In 2009, I became aware that my life was no longer normal when I found myself favoring a drug store in Frankfurt, a barber in Sweden, a florist in Berlin, and a pastry café in Buenos Aires—and don't forget the tailor in Bangkok. I draw my own maps as part of my diary to get a sense of where I am and where I am going next.

Clients appreciate the consultant's genuine interest in the communities in which the project develops and the local language and history.

When working with a major magazine in Paris, I reminisced with the project team about my French lessons in college.

With my German clients, I see the satisfaction on their faces when I sprinkle my presentations with some German terminology. I enrolled in an online German course–not seeking fluency but familiarity with the language. This allowed me to follow the conversations when the clients turned to their native German to discuss something I was presenting.

That was helpful. On a more playful note, I started peppering my presentation with terms such as *zwischentitel* (3) for those subheads that break up long masses of text in an article. Clients appreciate when the consultant winks at them!

PERSONAL NOTE
The Old Girl Still Had a Rumba Left in Her

On April 21, 2010, I wrote in my diary: I am here in Mendoza, overlooking the magnificent Andes. This area is where Argentina's top vineyards are situated. The world enjoys great red wines coming from Mendoza. My project here has a great in-house team, with many young journalists and designers eager to change the newspaper. What a blessing. But for the consultant, it is not all about what happens in the office. The lady selling candy out of a little kiosk in the Aconcagua Hotel lobby is friendly, early sixties, and her nickname is Chuchi.

I say good morning to her, and she notices that my Spanish is, as she put it, "Cuban-scented." That's all she needed to know to tell me that in her younger years here in Mendoza, she was the first dancer to do the Cuban rumba on stage.

She stepped out of the kiosk, in a blouse that displayed her bare shoulders, and told me that she still had her Cuban maracas. "I have always loved Cuban men," she said as she passed two or three pieces of sweet candy to me. "Try these, as sweet as Cuban sugarcane," she said flirtatiously. My driver was waiting outside •

Long after one forgets the details of the project itself, what one remembers are the little moments as when *The Candy Girl of the Aconcagua* appeared that morning—one of the perks of the traveling consultant.

It is not just the appearance of a colorful character that makes the day more interesting for the traveling consultant. Rather, it is the contact with regular people whose only relationship to the consultant's field is that they consume the product you are trying to improve. I use those opportunities as an informal focus group: "Do you read the daily newspaper here? What is your favorite section? What would you do differently if you were to change it?" Sometimes that ordinary person in the city contributes an extraordinary thought that none of the luminaries in the conference room, including the consultant, had thought about.

THE CONSULTANT OF THE FUTURE.
What a wonderful and fertile road ahead for consultants to grow and become even more essential as they help their clients achieve new levels of success, excellence, and profitability. And yet, the consultant of the future must meet more strict criteria than I did that fateful day in 1976 when my colleague John Zeien casually mentioned that there would be consulting in my future.

NEW SKILL SETS.
Usually, it is curiosity that leads us to acquiring new skills. It's more fun when you are eager to discover new ways of working as opposed to feeling an obligation to do so.

If I were starting my consulting journey today, I would need a diverse and advanced skill set to navigate the rapidly changing landscape of business and technology. These skills can be broadly categorized into technical, analytical, interpersonal, and adaptive abilities. I maintain that passion and heart will also be essentials, just like they have been for those of us who came before

TECHNOLOGICAL SKILLS.

Technology is a major part of what a consultant needs to understand and be well versed in. Technological skills the consultant must master include the following:

- **Digital literacy and technological proficiency:** Future consultants must be adept at leveraging technology to enhance business processes and drive innovation. This includes proficiency in data analytics, AI machine learning, and blockchain technologies.

- **Cybersecurity awareness:** With the increasing digitalization of businesses, cybersecurity has become paramount. Consultants need to understand cybersecurity principles to protect their clients' data and ensure compliance with regulations.

- **Expertise in digital transformation:** Consultants must guide organizations through digital transformation, helping them adopt new technologies and processes.

My own work as a consultant has involved major work assisting clients in the media making digital transformations, abandoning the print legacy. In this area, the consultant must incorporate an extra dose of diplomacy into his methodology. It is easy to lose your patience with clients who "don't get it" in terms of the realities of the new technology. My formula is to work with these editors individually. Let's do coffee or lunch, and, eventually, reason and reality prevail. The last thing the consultant wants to do is to embarrass these senior players in front of their more digitally savvy younger team members.

ANALYTICAL SKILLS.

A major portion of what consultants do is analyze data. Consultants should be proficient in using data analytics tools and techniques to identify trends, measure performance, and make informed decisions. This skill set is essential for providing evidence-based recommendations, and I recommend the following skills in this area, but be aware of new ones that be just as useful:

• **Advanced data analysis:** The ability to analyze complex datasets and extract actionable insights is crucial.

• **Strategic thinking:** Future consultants need to be strategic thinkers, capable of seeing the big picture while also paying attention to detail. This involves understanding market dynamics, competitive landscapes, and long-term business implications. Strategic thinking helps in developing comprehensive solutions that align with organizational goals. (4)

INTERPERSONAL SKILLS.

Consultants must be able to present their findings and recommendations to diverse audiences, including executives, stakeholders, and technical teams. I have always felt that my work as a college professor has been key as I synchronize it with my consulting work.

The ability to present ideas clearly is a major part of the success of a consulting project. Turn the conference room into a classroom, and everyone learns and appreciates you for the effort.

Effective communication is vital for conveying complex ideas in a clear and compelling manner. Storytelling techniques can help make data more relatable and persuasive. How we tell stories for consumption on mobile devices is key, and not just for journalists. Consultants can advance their ideas in writing more effectively by applying some of the basics for mobile storytelling. In my book **The Story,** I discuss in ample detail the need for crafting narratives that cater to the unique challenges and opportunities of small-screen consumption. One of the key elements of linear storytelling is that the text is created for vertical scrolling.

The narrative flows vertically, exactly as how we conduct a text or WhatsApp chat—we write and we show. Unlike the traditional structure, where text is uninterrupted and visuals appear by themselves, mobile storytelling often favors linear storytelling, where the story unfolds in a sequence designed to maintain user engagement. Stories are built for vertical scrolling, guiding readers step-by-step with a narrative arc that encourages them to continue reading.

Today, with so much consumption of content on mobile devices, it makes perfect sense for consultants to learn how we create content for mobile. In addition, because social media plays such an important role in our daily lives, with that comes an avalanche of first-person storytelling ("This is my new office," "Here I am vacationing in Maui," "Meet my new cat, Simon," etc.). All of this means that engaging your audience will happen faster and more efficiently if you personalize the presentation, especially at the beginning.

As consultants, we come in front of our clients with a basket of big ideas to present. It is our job to make sure that the clients not only understand those ideas but also adapt them to their work. It is all in the details: If I am doing a presentation for a company, I will make sure that the logo or avatar of that firm appears on all my slides. It is a handshake or a wink that says you are special, and I have prepared this thinking specifically of you. Think of the consultant addressing **Home Depot** managers who managed to get the iconic orange apron and bring it along.

Or let's say you are appearing in front of a group of high-level chefs whose performance will determine the future of a company. Rather than start with your five bullet points of what is needed, it might be better to personalize the start of the presentation: "Chef Wilson believes that food presentation is key, and she is proud of her artistic creations. Her colleague Chef Suarez considers decorations on a plate to be nothing more than culinary noise. Who is right?"

By now, you've already got the group engaged, and you can then proceed to expand on the importance of a variety of opinions to make good things happen. In mobile storytelling, our goal is to get readers to keep scrolling. In general presentations, our goal is to keep them engaged with our message.

ADAPTIVE SKILLS.
This type of more personalized storytelling involves being open to new ideas, quickly learning new skills, and adjusting strategies as needed. We have seen anecdotal evidence in this book about the importance of the consultant adapting to change, respecting and assimilating the culture of the client's environment, and learning at every step. Embracing a growth mindset allows consultants to navigate evolving industry

trends and client expectations with agility. Furthermore, cultivating strong interpersonal skills ensures effective collaboration and builds trust within diverse client ecosystems. The following two qualities are essential adaptive skills for the consultant:

• **Agility and flexibility:** The business environment is constantly evolving, and consultants must be adaptable to change. Agility allows consultants to respond effectively to unforeseen challenges and opportunities. (5)

• **Continuous learning and curiosity:** Consultants must continuously update their knowledge and skills to keep pace with technological advancements and industry trends. This requires a proactive approach to professional development and a genuine curiosity about emerging innovations. (6) It is also important to come ready to learn from the client and his team. I have often said that I could have received another graduate degree just for being exposed to so many bright minds and such a variety of experiences during my decades of consulting. I have learned about history and culture but also about the fervent pride and love that clients feel for their craft and where they work.

ETHICAL COMPETENCE.
Consultants must adhere to high ethical standards, ensuring that their advice and actions are in the best interest of their clients and society. This includes being transparent, accountable, and mindful of the broader impact of their work.

One time, a major competitor of a project that I had completed years before called to solicit my services. I turned it down, stating that I had been too involved with their major competitor. As I put it: "As a consultant to project X, I was in their kitchen for a year, and I know all their recipes. It would not be fair to get into your kitchen."

The prospective clients understood. And I shook my head, knowing that my company had lost a big chunk of change. Months later, the CEO of the project I had worked on called and told me that she knew that their competitor had reached out to me. "Not many people would do what you did, Mario," she told me. "And, by the way, we have a little project afoot here that we would like you to help us with." We all have to live with our choices, as in the proverbial "at peace with yourself when you rest your head on the pillow at night." Many of my existing projects come from repeat customers who appreciated the hard work, commitment to the goals of the project, and, most importantly, ethical behavior and respect for client confidentiality. I often say that the good consultant gets deep into the client's kitchen, which eliminates any ethical way of working with the client's competition.

CULTURAL COMPETENCE.
As businesses become more global, consultants need to understand and respect cultural differences. This skill helps in building strong relationships with international clients and working effectively in diverse environments. Cultural competence is crucial for fostering inclusive practices and promoting global collaboration.

MAKE A NOTE
The Consultant of the Future

The consultant of the future will be a technologically savvy, analytically sharp, and highly adaptive professional, equipped with advanced technical skills, strategic thinking, and strong interpersonal abilities. Continuous learning, ethical decision-making, and cultural competence will further enhance their capacity to drive meaningful change and deliver value to clients in a complex, fast-paced world. Be diplomatic and have tons of passion and an empathetic heart.

Conclusion

Reflecting on the Journey

The Second Birthday

Sixty-three years ago today, as I write this, I arrived in the United States as a Cuban refugee. That moment marked more than just a change in geography—it was the beginning of a new life, a new identity. To this day, I remain grateful to my parents for the choice they made, a decision that allowed me to become an American and build a future in a country that welcomed me. That is why I count February 28, 1962, as my second birthday. In a faded photograph, taken by my father that day, I stand on the tarmac in a pinstripe suit,

about to board a Pan Am flight to Miami. It was the last time I stood on Cuban soil. A new Mario was forced to be born that day. I remember that particular Wednesday with remarkable clarity—one of the few days in my life that remains etched in my memory, nearly hour by hour. I woke up at home in Havana, nerves tightening in my stomach, the excitement of the unknown mixing with the sadness of leaving behind my parents, my language, and the only life I had ever known.

"It is time to go," my father said, his voice steady, though I knew he was pretending to sip his morning café Cubano to mask his emotions. My mother was uncharacteristically silent. I carried more than just memories with me on that flight. The yellow hairs of our cat, Simon, clung stubbornly to my pants, hitching a ride across the Florida Straits. I had little else—just three changes of clothing, the maximum allowed by the Cuban government for those leaving the country.

That day, I was no longer just Mario, the Cuban boy. I was Mario, the refugee. And from that moment on, I would have to earn everything anew—starting as a busboy in a Miami restaurant, struggling to learn English, working tirelessly to try to get my parents a visa to join me in the US, and, in the process, becoming a mature adult at fourteen.

WHY THIS BOOK?

After finishing my most recent book, **AI: The Next Revolution in Content Creation**, I thought I was done writing. But books have a way of pulling you back in, demanding to be written.

This one is no exception. After decades as a consultant, guiding companies and individuals through transformation, I feel compelled to share my experiences—the lessons, the challenges, the stories that shaped my career. This book is a reflection on what it means to advise, to lead, and to navigate the ever-changing landscape of business and media. I hope that in these pages, both seasoned professionals and aspiring consultants will find useful techniques, inspiration, and the ability to imagine what could be, and never stop dreaming. In many ways, I am still that boy in the pinstripe suit—stepping into the unknown, ready to begin again.

THE LONG ROAD.

As I look back on my fifty-five-plus years as a consultant, with 760 projects across 122 countries, I can't help but marvel at what a journey it has been. This life of travel and meeting extraordinary people on six continents has been nothing short of incredible. It's difficult to separate my biography from the trajectory of my career because they are so intertwined. Since 1976, I've had the same passion for my projects and clients as I did when I first started.

My journey began modestly, traveling in a vintage 1970s Chevrolet station wagon through the snowy hills of upstate New York to small regional newspapers that sought a design consultant. I was stepping into newsrooms with a fresh perspective, eager to transform the way stories were told and consumed. Over the years, I have become more than just a consultant. I have been a father confessor, a facilitator, a hand-holder, and an interpreter of dreams for my clients. I had no previous preparation for any of these roles, but, believe me, once you are on the job, it all comes naturally. My role has always been to bridge the gap between vision and execution, to empower clients, and to be an agent of change. When arriving at a new project, change is in the air, and change is wanted, although not necessarily by all the players. Therein lies the challenge.

Every project, every client, has been unique. Whether working with a major newspaper in New York, a burgeoning digital platform in Delhi, or a traditional print outlet in Buenos Aires, the challenge was always the same: to understand the unique needs and dreams of each client and to help turn those dreams into reality. I've seen the evolution of media from print to digital, from desktop to mobile, and I have been privileged to help navigate these transformations. Passion and belief in myself, my craft, and the people I was working with guided the journey.

Unlike people who spend their entire career in one office, one firm, or one institution, I've become a citizen of the planet. I may visit three different clients in three different countries within the span of a week or a month. I remember the days when I would have breakfast in Frankfurt, lunch in Vienna, and dinner in Paris. This has required me to change gears and adapt to different languages, cultures, and methodologies, weaving a rich tapestry of not only my craft but also the human condition. I've learned to appreciate the subtle nuances of different cultures and the universal language of storytelling.

I have also learned that even the most highly placed stakeholders of a project have the same fears and insecurities that the rest of us have. Perhaps the most useful phrase a consultant can utter is "Everything is going to be all right." It works the same for the CEO in charge of changing gears and pushing the company's profits up as for the designer at the bottom of the roster who doubts her talent and abilities and fears that a new project will threaten her job.

Reflecting on this incredible journey, I wouldn't change a single day of my consulting career. There were many moments of bliss and, of course, rejection. Overall, my memories accentuate the positive. Maybe that's why, at seventy-eight, I still travel the world, interpreting dreams—and even have new dreams of my own.

I never set out to be a consultant, but, oh, am I ever lucky to have become one. Each project and each client has enriched my life in ways I could never have imagined. The friendships I've formed, the stories I've heard—many of which I have shared with you here—and the dreams I've helped realize have all been part of this extraordinary tapestry. The fourteen-year-old Cuban refugee who always lives inside of me is grateful for the journey; one I have never taken for granted. I extend my gratitude to every client who ever put their faith in me. More importantly, I express my love and eternal gratitude to my late wife, Maria, and my four children for allowing me to follow my heart and passion. So, you want to be a consultant . . .

Prepare yourself for an exciting and personally rewarding journey, and let those two essentials, your passion and heart, carry you along the way. You won't regret it.

Notes

CHAPTER 1

1. **Roger Black,** email to the author, July 15, 2024.
2. **IBISWorld,** "Global Management Consultants–Employment (2005–2031)," last updated December 2024, https://www.ibisworld.com/global/employment/global-management-consultants/1950/.
3. **Spherical Insights,** "Global Consulting Service Market Size to Be Worth USD 494.36 Billion by 2033 | CAGR Of 4.20%," GlobeNewswire, April 17, 2024, https://www.globenewswire.com/news-release/2024/04/17/2864897/0/en/Global-Consulting-Service-Market-Size-To-Worth-USD-494-36-Billion-By-2033-CAGR-Of-4-20.html?utm_source=chatgpt.com.
4. **Iryna Viter,** "The Ultimate List of Consulting Statistics, Trends & Facts for 2025," Runn, January 11, 2023, https://www.runn.io/blog/consulting-statistics; IBISWorld, "Global Management Consultants–Employment (2005–2031)," last updated December 2024, https://www.ibisworld.com/global/number-of-businesses/global-management-consultants/1950/.
5. **Samir Parikh,** *The Consultant's Handbook* (Wiley, 2015, Kindle), 6.
6. **Linda K. Stroh,** *The Basic Principles of Effective Consulting* (Routledge, 2005), 3.
7. **Alan Weiss,** *The Consulting Bible: How to Launch and Grow a Seven-Figure Consulting Business* (Wiley, 2021).
8. **Rick Tetzeli,** "The Creative Process Is Fabulously Unpredictable. A Great Idea Cannot Be Predicted," *McKinsey Quarterly,* McKinsey & Company, June 2023, https://www.mckinsey.com/capabilities/mckinsey-digital/our-insights/the-creative-process-is-fabulously-unpredictable-a-great-idea-cannot-be-predicted.
9. **Weiss,** *The Consulting Bible,* 96.
10. **Weiss,** *The Consulting Bible,* 96.

CHAPTER 2

1. **Read the study where readers commented** on the replacement of the *St. Cloud Daily Times'* eagle in the newspaper's logo. Mario García, J.W. Click, and Guido Stempel III, "Reader Response to Redesign of *St. Cloud Daily Times," Newspaper Research Journal* 2, no. 2 (Winter 1981), https://www.proquest.com/openview/888ebecaa6dd2cbab0963be72b3436e7/1?pq-origsite=gscholar&cbl=1821490.

CHAPTER 3

1. **David Maister,** Charles Green, and Robert Galford, *The Trusted Advisor* (Free Press, 2021).
2. **Margarita Moreno,** personal interview, September 7, 2024.
3. **Moreno,** personal interview, September 7, 2024.
4. **Moreno,** personal interview, September 7, 2024.

CHAPTER 4

1. **Josh Tapper,** "Getting Lapped by Innovation Abroad? Mario Garcia's Path to Better Designed Newspapers," *NiemanLab*, November 1, 2010, https://www.niemanlab.org/2010/11/getting-lapped-by-innovation-abroad-mario-garcias-path-to-better-designed-newspapers/.

CHAPTER 5

1. **Source Global Research,** "How Consultants Can Build More Trust in Their Client Relationships," December 13, 2021, https://www.sourceglobalresearch.com/blog-post/how-consultants-can-build-more-trust-in-their-client-relationships-2.
2. **Alan Weiss,** *The Consulting Bible: How to Launch and Grow a Seven-Figure Consulting Business* (Wiley, 2021), 7.
3. **Mario García, "Redesigning The Wall Street Journal,"** *The Wall Street Journal*, April 11, 2000, https://www.wsj.com/articles/SB955398654498473035; **"Q&A: Mario Garcia Explains Design of the New Nameplate,"** The Wall Street Journal, September 19, 2005, https://www.wsj.com/articles/SB112713856091444866; **Pegie Stark, "Behind the Redesign: WSJ,"** P*oynter,* August 1, 2002, https://www.poynter.org/archive/2002/behind-the-redesign-wsj/; **"Journal Redesigns Banner for International Editions,"** *The Wall Street Journal*, September 20, 2005, https://www.wsj.com/articles/SB112716369675745304.

CHAPTER 6

1. **Edward Tufte,** *The Visual Display of Quantitative Information* (Graphics Press, 2001).
2. **Nigel Holmes,** nigelholmes.com.
3. **Tony Buzan,** *The Mind Map Book* (BBC Active, 2010).
4. **"SWOT Analysis,"** The Decision Lab, https://thedecisionlab.com/reference-guide/management/swot-analysis.
5. **Edward de Bono,** *Six Thinking Hats* (Little, Brown and Company, 1985).
6. **Roger Black,** email correspondence with author, July 15, 2024.

CHAPTER 7

1. **Peter Block,** *Flawless Consulting: A Guide to Getting Your Expertise Used* (Wiley, 2023).
2. **Block,** *Flawless Consulting.*

CHAPTER 8

1. **Sandeep Krishnan,** *The Mind of a Consultant: Leveraging a Consulting Mindset for Professional Success* (Portfolio, 2021), 28.
2. **Krishnan,** *The Mind of a Consultant,* 196.
3. **Margarita Moreno,** personal interview, September 8, 2024.
4. **Krishnan,** *The Mind of a Consultant,* 53.
5. **Delphine d'Amora,** "City Hall Buys Weekly Paper to Extend 'Reach,'" **The Moscow Times**, March 12, 2014, https://www.themoscowtimes.com/2014/03/12/city-hall-buys-weekly-paper-to-extend-reach-a32908.

Notes

CHAPTER 9

1. **Alan Weiss,** *The Consulting Bible: How to Launch and Grow a Seven-Figure Consulting Business* (Wiley, 2021), 66.
2. **Andreas Kaplan and Michael Haenlein,** "Users of the World, Unite! The Challenges and Opportunities of Social Media," *Business Horizons* 53, no. 1 (January–February 2010): 59–68, https://doi.org/10.1016/j.bushor.2009.09.003.
3. **Sonja Gensler, Franziska Völckner, Yuping Liu-Thompkins, and Caroline Wiertz,** "Managing Brands in the Social Media Environment," *Journal of Interactive Marketing* 27, no. 4 (November 2013): 242–56, https://doi.org/10.1016/j.intmar.2013.09.004.
4. **Michael Zipursky and Daryl Bates-Brownsword,** "The Truth about Selling Your Consulting Business," October 27, 2024, in *The Consulting Success Podcast,* podcast, https://www.consultingsuccess.com/the-truth-about-selling-your-consulting-business-with-darryl-bates-brownsword-podcast-339.
5. **Gerald Weinberg,** *The Secrets of Consulting: A Guide to Giving and Getting Advice Successfully* (Dorset House Publishing, 1985), 2.
6. **Sylvia Plath,** *The Unabridged Journals of Sylvia Plath* (Anchor Books, 1982), 545.

CHAPTER 10

1. **Ethan Mollick,** *Co-Intelligence: Living and Working with AI* (Penguin, 2024), 66–67.
2. **Mario García,** *AI: The Next Revolution in Content Creation* (Thane & Prose, 2023), 16.
3. **Fabrizio Dell'Acqua et al.,** "Navigating the Jagged Technological Frontier: Field Experimental Evidence of the Effects of AI on Knowledge Worker Productivity and Quality," Working paper 24-013, Harvard Business School, September 22, 2023, https://www.hbs.edu/ris/Publication%20Files/24-013_d9b45b68-9e74-42d6-a1c6-c72fb70c7282.pdf.
4. **Anil Doshi and Oliver Hauser,** "Generative Artificial Intelligence Enhances Creativity but Reduces the Diversity of Novel Content," *Science Advances* 10, no. 28, August 8, 2023, http://dx.doi.org/10.2139/ssrn.4535536.
5. **Erik Brynjolfsson, Danielle Li, and Lindsey Raymond,** "Generative AI at Work," Working paper 31161, National Bureau of Economic Research, April 2023, https://www.nber.org/papers/w31161.
6. **Dell'Acqua, et al.,** "Navigating the Jagged Technological Frontier."
7. **Dell'Acqua, et al.,** "Navigating the Jagged Technological Frontier."
8. **Mollick,** *Co-Intelligence,* 181.
9. **Sophie Kahn,** "Sophie Kahn," *Coeval Magazine,* October 14, 2021, https://www.coeval-magazine.com/coeval/sophie-kahn?utm_source=chatgpt.com.
10. **Brian Christian,** *The Alignment Problem: Machine Learning and Human Values* (W.W. Norton & Company, 2020).
11. **Iryna Viter,** "The Ultimate List of Consulting Statistics, Trends & Facts for 2025," Runn, January 11, 2023, runn.io/blog/consulting-statistics.
12. **Viter,** "The Ultimate List of Consulting."
13. **Viter,** "The Ultimate List of Consulting."
14. **Viter,** "The Ultimate List of Consulting."
15. **Leonard Boussioux et al.,** The Crowdless Future? How Generative AI Is Shaping the Future of Human Crowdsourcing (SSRN, 2023).

CHAPTER 11

1. **Shannon Liao,** "This Harry Potter AI-Generated Fanfiction Is Remarkably Good," *The Verge*, December 12, 2017, https://www.theverge.com/2017/12/12/16768582/harry-potter-ai-fanfiction.
2. **Melanie Clegg et al.,** "HumanMachine Creativity–How AI Can Influence Human Creativity in Open Innovation," *Marketing Review St. Gallen* 39, no. 6 (June 2022): 40–47, https://www.econstor.eu/bitstream/10419/279711/1/MRSG_2022_6_40-47.pdf.
3. **Sandeep Krishnan,** *The Mind of a Consultant: Leveraging a Consulting Mindset for Professional Success* (Portfolio, 2021), 40.
4. **Federica Laricchia,** "Brands of Tablets Owned in the United States in 2024," Statista, July 3, 2024, https://www.statista.com/statistics/1474707/tablet-ownership-by-brand-us.
5. **Mario García,** *iPad Design Lab - Basic: Storytelling in the Age of the Tablet* (Adams Media, 2012).
6. **Mario García,** *The Story: Transformation, Storytelling and Design in the Mobile News Movement* (Thane & Prose, 2019).
7. **Mario García,** *AI: The Next Revolution in Content Creation* (Thane & Prose, 2024).

CHAPTER 12

1. **"Die Zeit, Weekendavisen and The New York Times Named World's Best Designed,"** Society for New Design, May 17, 2024, https://snd.org/die-zeit-weekendavisen-and-the-new-york-times-named-worlds-best-designed/.
2. **From email interview with Emory Thomas**, *American Cities Business Journal*, July 29, 2024.
3. ***Zwischentitel* is a German word that translates to "intertitle" in English.** It can refer to a title card in a film or video or a chapter heading in a typographical work.
4. **Sherwin Chua,** "Eight Big Ideas for Newsroom Transformation and Digital Revenue Growth," World Association of News Publishers, October 27, 2020, https://wan-ifra.org/2020/10/eight-big-ideas-for-newsroom-transformation-and-digital-revenue-growth/.
5. **Brent Gleeson,** "The 7 Ways to Respond to Constant Change with Agility and Adaptability," *Forbes*, November 20, 2023, https://www.forbes.com/sites/brentgleeson/2023/11/20/the-7-ways-to-respond-to-constant-change-with-agility-and-adaptability/.
6. **Lucy Kueng,** "Media Leaders Must Keep Learning. Here Are Five Principles to Guide Your Own Learning and Ensure It Delivers," Reuters Institute, December 20, 2024, https://reutersinstitute.politics.ox.ac.uk/news/media-leaders-must-keep-learning-here-are-five-principles-guide-your-own-learning-and-ensure?Institute_for_the_Study_of_Journalism=&utm_term=0_-1eb74b9098-101273481.

Image Credits

About the Author

Dr. Mario R. García is senior advisor on News Design and adjunct professor at Columbia University's School of Journalism. He is also the CEO/founder of **García Media**, a global consulting firm. He has been involved with the redesign and rethinking of more than 750 publications in 120 countries, including **The Wall Street Journal** and **The Washington Post**. He came to the School of Journalism as the Hearst Digital Media Professional in Residence in 2013. He is the author of sixteen books and continues to work with newsrooms across the world. He has been involved with The Poynter Institute's EyeTrack Research since its inception, including the EyeTrack: Tablet. His awards include a Lifetime Achievement Award from the Society for News Design and The Journalism Medal of Honor from the University of Missouri for Distinguished Service in Journalism. In 2015, Mario became the recipient of the Columbia Scholastic Press Association's Charles O'Malley Excellence in Teaching Award. **People** magazine mentioned him among the one hundred most influential Hispanics in the United States. He received his PhD from the University of Miami. Today, Mario is totally engaged in mobile-first storytelling and AI and the transformation of news and information across digital platforms. *Follow TheMarioBlog at garciamedia.com.*

Reactions

"Mario García has crafted more than just a book about consulting. García has penned an essential life manual for anyone who seeks to blend professional excellence with profound humanity. He reminds us that the most impactful lessons are not found in textbooks but in the rich tapestry of human interaction. This book is a powerful testament to the idea that true influence stems from a place of passion, empathy, and unwavering integrity. A compelling and inspiring read for anyone dedicated to making a meaningful difference in their field."

ULRIK JUUL CHRISTENSEN, MD
Globally recognized authority in learning technology, known for his
pioneering work in adaptive learning, data-driven content development.

"Mario García does everything with energy, passion and intelligence —including writing this book, which tells how he does everything with energy, passion and intelligence. It's the framework for what has been a successful career for him—and could be for anyone else who follows his good advice."

MARCUS BRAUCHLI
Journalist, media investor, and advisor.
Former editor of *The Washington Post, The Wall Street Journal*.

"Reading this book, we see what makes a great design consultant: A great story. Mario is the master storyteller, and along the way, he has carried narratives to clients that they will always remember."

ROGER BLACK
Typographer, 20th-century magazine designer, founder of one of the early desktop
type design studios, Font Bureau (1989), and current chairman of Type Network.

"[*Consulting with Heart*] offers a lot for individuals who want to become consultants. García's experience and expertise come through as well as concrete advice for now and the future."

RAJU NARISETTI
Journalist and former newspaper editor, global publishing
director at McKinsey & Company since 2020.

www.ingramcontent.com/pod-product-compliance
Lightning Source LLC
Chambersburg PA
CBHW040918210326
41597CB00030B/5120